THE
SECRET OF PASCAL

THE
SECRET OF PASCAL,

BY

H. F. STEWART.

Locuta est Dalila ad Samson:
Dic mihi, obsecro, in quo sit tua maxima fortitudo.

CAMBRIDGE

AT THE UNIVERSITY PRESS

1941

CAMBRIDGE UNIVERSITY PRESS
Cambridge, New York, Melbourne, Madrid, Cape Town,
Singapore, São Paulo, Delhi, Tokyo, Mexico City

Cambridge University Press
The Edinburgh Building, Cambridge CB2 8RU, UK

Published in the United States of America by Cambridge University Press, New York

www.cambridge.org
Information on this title: www.cambridge.org/9780521237802

First published 1941
First paperback edition 2011

A catalogue record for this publication is available from the British Library

ISBN 978-0-521-23780-2 Paperback

A LA FRANCE,
QUAND MÊME

CONTENTS

These few pages are to be regarded as a postscript to the brief homiletic volume which I put out in 1915 under the title—for want of a better—*The Holiness of Pascal*. Twenty-five years of constant practice and consequent intimacy have not led me to change my opinion with regard to his religious thought and attitude. Pascal, for me, retains his halo of sanctity.

But there are other aspects of his genius, and I have felt moved, before I disappear, to submit my thoughts upon three of them to the judgment of an English audience—his skill in debate, his moral teaching, and his mastery of language. Divinity and religion will keep breaking in, but on the whole I have tried to confine myself to a secular standpoint. Other and very important fields are here neglected—his mathematics, his science, and his philosophy—for want of time and want of competence; but I venture to hope that by these two small books I may have been able to do something to justify and explain the interest so widely felt in this singular figure. I do not say, to awaken it. For indeed his hold upon the imagination and affection of thoughtful men of every race and every clime remains unbroken by the changes and chances of human experience.

The title which I have chosen may be deemed too ambitious for so tenuous an effort as this, but I feel that somewhere in the regions which it touches the answer will be found to the question, What is the secret of Pascal?★

Of the three chapters, much of the first has already appeared in the *Festschrift* in honour of Sir Herbert Grierson which the Clarendon Press published in 1939; the other two are new.

As in the former volume, I have added a sheaf of explanatory and referential notes.

The frontispiece is taken from the death-mask which is the origin of all existing portraits of Pascal, except Domat's chalk drawing of him as a youth.

The numeration of the *Pensées* is that of Léon Brunschvicg's edition, which has become classical.

H. F. STEWART

December 1940

★ *Vide infra*, p. 102.

CHAPTER I

Pascal in Debate

Pascal's brief and fevered life was rich in controversy.
That, when we consider his character, training, and
opportunities, was to be expected. An eager, in-
quisitive child, who *would* know the why and
wherefore of everything, refused to be put off with
easy answer, and, when baulked, found out a way
for himself[1]—a youth stubborn in the protection of
what seemed to him sound doctrine[2]—a scientific
genius, jealous of the rights of his discoveries and
inventions[3]—a friend responding readily and reck-
lessly, with all his gifts of heart and head, to the call
for help,[4] but turning fiercely on his teachers when
he deemed them traitors to the truth[5]—a master of
logic and language, loud of voice and formidable
of mien[6]—such was Pascal. He was much else besides; but these are features which mark him as
likely to plunge into a fight and win it, whenever
occasion arose. And it arose early.

In 1647, when he was twenty-four years old, a
fresh-minted Jansenist (the conversion of his whole
family to that body of doctrine was in 1646), there

appeared at Rouen, where his father held a high position in the Inland Revenue, a personage of unusual interest and singular notions, Jacques Forton, sieur de Saint-Ange.[7] He had recently quitted the Capuchin Order and was come into Normandy seeking a benefice, armed with papal dispensation and royal letters patent. His reputation or notoriety as philosopher and public lecturer inspired Pascal and some like-minded companions with a desire to see him and hear him; and he was glad to satisfy their curiosity. Two meetings were arranged early in February at which Saint-Ange expounded his views. They sounded strange to these young Augustinians, amateurs of theology and natural science; they included a restatement of the heresy of Ramon Lull, viz. that man can by the mere exercise of reason attain comprehension of the Trinity and all the mysteries of the Faith;[8] a definition of the Humanity of Our Lord and of His mother as a separate and peculiar Creation (this it may be remarked was especially shocking to Pascal,[9] though it contains the germ of the doctrine of the Immaculate Conception); subtle distinctions between sanctifying and ministerial Grace; the meaning of "libre" and "liberté", and so on. There were also physical speculations about the age of the earth and the number of its inhabitants, calculable by its cubic

mass. Saint-Ange's divinity, and his science so far
as it affected his divinity, seemed so hazardous,
especially in a priest and teacher, that the young men,
while they openly laughed at his extravagances, considered themselves bound to denounce them to
ecclesiastical authority, to wit François de Harlay,
archbishop of Rouen and J.-P. Camus, his co-
adjutor. Neither of these dignitaries was inclined
to take the matter seriously; they were satisfied with
vague protestations of orthodoxy on the part of
Saint-Ange. But the self-appointed inquisitors
were insistent; further and closer enquiry was made,
and at the end of two months Jacques Forton with-
drew a dozen doubtful propositions advanced by
him in the course of his conversations, and was
permitted to proceed to a living, that of Crosville
in the deanery of Bacqueville. But the accusation,
despite the recantation, created such a prejudice
against him that he never took possession. Odium
pursued him to the benefice near Pontoise which he
obtained by exchange, and so, unfortunate victim
of a heresy-hunt, he fades out of sight.

The interest of the incident lies for us in Pascal's
revulsion against a theory which exalts Reason
above Faith, the high hand with which he evidently
conducted the debate, and the fact that he borrows
from the captive of his dialectic and reproduces in

more than one passage the very form in which Forton cast the familiar philosophic tenet that truth lies in a reconciliation of contraries.[10] He regarded the field of knowledge as common property and was not above taking a lesson from a foe.

The "affaire Saint-Ange" was but an interlude in the midst of serious scientific experiments on the Torricellian vacuum with which Blaise and his father were busy in the early months of 1647, and which Blaise and his brother-in-law, M. Périer, carried to a triumphant conclusion by means of simultaneous observations from the top of the Puy de Dôme and the Tour Saint-Jacques la Boucherie in Paris on 19 September 1648. Henceforth it was established beyond reach of doubt that the gap between the column of mercury and the end of the tube was not filled with "matière subtile" as Descartes posited, but was verily and indeed empty space, due to the pressure of the atmosphere.

The Rouen experiments preliminary to the final proof were described by Pascal in a pamphlet of thirty-six pages which he dedicated to his father and published in October 1647,[11] promising a fuller treatise by and by.

This brought him into touch with the body which was presently to exercise his dialectic, in the person of le Père Noël, S.J., rector of the Jesuit college of

Clermont. This old gentleman (he was sixty-six),
a friend of Descartes whom he had taught at La
Flèche (whose disbelief in the existence of a vacuum
he shared though, unlike the philosopher, he clung
to Aristotelian doctrine and tried to make it square
with modern science), wrote to Pascal a rather
patronising but quite friendly letter about his
pamphlet, praising it, but begging leave to doubt
the "vide apparent qui paraît dans le tube après la
descente soit de l'eau soit du vif argent. Je dis que
c'est un corps" etc. And he proceeds to argue with
little science and less logic in favour of subtle matter
filtering through the pores of the glass. Noël's
science is borrowed from Aristotle, but his logic is
his own.

Pascal, in a long and courteous reply, dated
29 October 1647, gives him a lesson in both. For
instance, Noël defines light in these terms: "La
lumière est un mouvement luminaire des rayons,
composés des corps lucides qui remplissent les corps
transparents." Upon which Pascal remarks: "Il me
semble qu'il faudrait avoir premièrement défini ce
que c'est que *luminaire*, et ce que c'est que corps
lucide ou *lumineux*: car jusque là je ne puis entendre
ce que c'est que lumière. Et comme nous n'em-
ployons jamais dans les définitions le terme du
défini, j'aurais peine à m'accommoder à la vôtre,

qui dit que la *lumière* est un mouvement *luminaire des corps lumineux*" (the italics are Pascal's). This ludicrous definition remained in his mind. Ten years later, in 1658, he reproduces it in his *Réflexions sur l'esprit géométrique*, and in the *Art de persuader*, which follows it, he lays down the rule, neglect of which had led Father Noël to talk nonsense: "Voilà en quoi consiste cet art de persuader, qui se renferme dans ces deux principes: définir tous les noms qu'on impose; prouver tout, en substituant mentalement les définitions à la place des définis." If he failed to induce the living Jesuit to accept this maxim he had no difficulty in winning acceptance for it on the part of the imaginary Jesuit of the fourth Provincial letter: "Vous voulez", says he, "que je substitue la définition au défini; cela ne change jamais le sens du discours; je le veux bien."

A second letter from Noël, longer and less intelligible than the first, was left unanswered until it was suggested to Pascal that silence would be taken to mean defeat. So he wrote an elaborate reply, not to Noël himself, perhaps for fear of further correspondence, but to their common friend M. Le Pailleur. These two letters do more than correct particular blunders of the Jesuit father; they lay down laws of logical debate and form a little manual of methodology which it had been well if

not only Père Noël, but all the members of his
society, had laid to heart.[12] Indeed, they needed all
their logic to meet the formidable onslaught which
Pascal made upon them in the *Provincial Letters*
from January 1656 to May 1657.

These letters are immortal through their wit and
eloquence. "Les meilleurs comédies de Molière
n'ont pas plus de sel que les premières *Provinciales*;
Bossuet n'a rien de plus sublime que les dernières."
So wrote Voltaire, no friend of Pascal's, and we
have no difficulty in endorsing his opinions. But
Attic salt is not the sole preservative against the
decay that threatens all human writings; nor can
mere eloquence rekindle the ashes of a dead controversy. The letters are alive to-day by reason of
their marvellous dialectic, their sheer force of
thought. That dialectic gathers strength as the
business proceeds, and it reaches its climax in the
last three letters; but Pascal was master of his
instrument from the outset, and the skirmish with
Père Noël, ten years before, shews how little he
had to learn of the way to conduct debate.[13]

Let us start from the beginning, the first letter,
dated 23 January 1656; or better still, let us slip into
the parlour at Port-Royal des Champs one afternoon
in January where "ces messieurs" are gathered, an
anxious company, considering what to do in the

matter of Antoine Arnauld's examination by the
Sorbonne on a charge of "temerity", if not of
actual heresy. He had publicly defended Jansen and
denied that the five propositions condemned by
Rome were contained in his book, the *Augustinus*.[14]
Nay he had, in an open letter addressed to a Duke
and Peer, who had been accused of Jansenism,[15]
gone so far as to repeat the first proposition, viz.
that Grace, the Grace necessary for action, could
fail a saint, and had in fact once failed a saint, to wit,
St Peter when he denied his Master. This doing, he
put his hand into a hornet's nest. It was to no
purpose that he quoted St Augustine in support of
his statement, and pleaded that the Pope himself
had approved of his letter. His enemies in the
Faculty of Theology were bent on his undoing, and
the way in which they handled his affair shewed
clearly that he was in grave danger of censure,
degradation, and loss of his Sorbonne fellowship.
In spite of his cleverness and readiness to compromise there was no chance of his winning his case.
His Latin pamphlets[16] fell on deaf ears; his friends
felt that the only hope was to appeal to a wider and
unprejudiced audience. Pierre Nicole, who was
present at the conference of Arnauld's friends,
describes the situation and the very scene: "The
Sorbonne was busy examining M. Arnauld's second

letter with the resultant commotion of which we are all aware. Those who did not know what it was all about, imagined that it was a question of the foundations of the Faith, or at least of something extremely important for religion. . . . One day when Montalte [Pascal's pseudonym] was conversing as usual with some of his friends, they chanced to mention their feelings at the way in which people were being put upon who were incapable of forming judgment on these disputes which they would have condemned had they been able to do so. All present agreed that the matter deserved attention and that it was desirable to open men's eyes. Whereupon some one remarked that the way to effect this was to put out a pamphlet showing that nothing serious or important was involved in these disputes, but merely a question of words, and of a simple chicane, turning on equivocal terms which they refused to explain. This notion was generally approved, but no one offered to put it into execution. Then Montalte, who hitherto had hardly written anything, and was unaware of the success he could have in this sort of writing, said that he thought he saw how this pamphlet could be written, but that he could only promise to sketch it in outline and leave it to another to polish and make fit for publication. . . . He set about next day working at what he had promised. But instead of a sketch he wrote out of hand the first letter just as we have it. He passed it on to one of his friends, who determined to have it printed at once, which was duly done."[17]

Pascal was indeed well equipped for the task imposed upon him and gladly accepted. He knew little or no theology; but he knew an equivocal term when he saw it. He also knew the world—he had spent eighteen months in Vanity Fair—and how to deal with its denizens; and this he proceeds to do with vigour.

The first two of his letters are a demonstration of the way to treat equivocal terms. There was the good scholastic term, *proxima potestas*, "pouvoir prochain",[18] which Dominicans and Jesuits agreed to use for their own purpose, viz. the discomfiture of Arnauld, although they were not at one as to its meaning; there is "Sufficient Grace" which upon investigation proves to be insufficient; there is "Actual Grace" which is a mere shibboleth. How are these ambiguities to be cleared up? Pascal knew how, and he attained his object with a stroke of the pen—what Nicole styles his unaccustomed pen.

The effect of the first letter was stunning. "Cette pièce", notes in his diary M. de Saint-Gilles, one of the Solitaries, "a un débit et un applaudissement merveilleux, et comme elle expose agréablement l'ignorance et les contradictions des Molinistes, elle les fâche beaucoup."[19]

Chancellor Séguier, the Jesuits' friend and protector, who presided with sovran partiality over the meetings of the Sorbonne, was threatened with a fit of apoplexy at his first reading, and had to be bled seven times by way of safeguard. But the Society itself, despite its vexation, kept quiet. Willing to defend doctrine when assailed, they were content to suffer slander patiently. So they said; but that did not prevent them from calling in the help of the civil arm to stop the flow of these anonymous and unprivileged pamphlets. All in vain. Blow fell upon blow. The letters followed each other in more or less rapid succession until by July 1656 they had mounted up to nine. Still the Jesuits held their fire, apart from a few insignificant fly-sheets and continued attempts at suppression. Then in August, simultaneously with the tenth letter, "finding their patience and modest silence being used against them, they felt that the public must have an antidote to these infamous writings". The antidote took the form of a *Première Réponse aux Lettres que les Jansénistes publient contre les pères de la Compagnie de Jésus, par un père de la même compagnie*, followed by a *Seconde Réponse* consisting of twenty-nine *Impostures*, together with separate replies to Letters XI to XVIII as they came out. The chief author of all these counterstrokes was Jacques Nouet, professor of Rhetoric at the Jesuit college, who was under the impression that he was dealing with Arnauld himself, a former subject of his attack over the *Fréquente Communion*.[20] To Nouet was presently joined the famous preacher Brisacier, and finally the redoubtable Père Annat, keeper of the King's conscience.

Pascal meets their accusations with counter-charges, and every stroke draws blood. I think of Alan Breck, driving the crew of the *Covenant* before him along the deck: "The sword in his hand flashed like quick-silver into the middle of our flying enemies, and at every flash came the scream of a man hurt."[21]

Two years later, in 1659, the *Réponses* were honoured by a translation into English,[22] in which the anonymous translator tried to arrange them in a somewhat better order than the original. But whether in French or English, they are poor stuff. Pascal had little difficulty in demolishing their flimsy argument, and he was flushed with victory when he let the sword fall from his hand in April or May 1657.[23]

Their flimsy argument! The Jesuits commit every possible sin against logic. This is best seen by

a "travail de contre-parties" in which, following
good scholastic precedent, we set their logic in face
of Pascal's.

The head and front of their offending is the
petitio principii, to which they have constant resort,
assuming as certain what is not certain and requires
proof. For instance, addressing the writer, they
say: "Vous êtes hérétique, personne ne vous croira
pas, tandis que nous avons du crédit auprès tout
le monde, à la réserve des hérétiques et de leurs
complices"—which is beside the point and a
gratuitous assumption at that.

Again: "On sait de bonne part que les Jansénistes
ont voulu corrompre par argent les savants
docteurs de Sorbonne pour enseigner leurs erreurs
dans l'école"—a gratuitous assumption accom-
panied by a gratuitous slander.

Again: "Celui qui écrit les Lettres est de Port-
Royal; le Port-Royal est déclaré hérétique; donc
celui qui écrit les Lettres est déclaré hérétique"—
another assumption; Nouet assumes that Arnauld
was the author of the letters; but he makes no
attempt to prove it.

Before passing to Pascal's logic, a word must be
said about his stout denial that he was "of Port-
Royal",[24] which is commonly regarded as an equivocation, if not a downright lie. The fact is that

"être de Port-Royal" was almost a technical term.
The Solitaries, of whom Antoine Arnauld was the
chief, were generally said and understood to be "of
Port-Royal", having renounced the world for a
religious life and the shelter of the convent. Now
Pascal, when he wrote the *Provinciales*, had by no
means renounced the world; he was still an "honn-
nête homme" in the seventeenth-century sense of
the word. The Solitaries regarded him as a friend
indeed, but not as one of their inner circle. Fontaine,
their historian, expressly distinguishes him from
"les Messieurs".[25] He was devoted to them; he
was fighting for them, but he was no more "of
them" than, say, the Duc de Luynes, the patron and
protector of Port-Royal, who would have been
unwilling to accept the appellation.

Now for his logic. He very rarely falls into the
snare of the *petitio principii*. "Prove what you assert;
I prove what I assert", is his constant cry. "Voyons
donc comment vous prouvez ce que vous dites; et
vous verrez ensuite comment je prouve ce que je
dis" (*Lettre* XIII).

There was, however, one occasion when he
slipped and let himself be dragged into a gratuitous
assumption; and that was at the point in the fifth
letter where he describes the motives by which he
holds the Society to be actuated. "Their object",

he says, "is not to corrupt morals; that is not their
purpose. But neither is their sole aim the improve-
ment of morals. They have such a good opinion of
themselves that they think it useful and almost
necessary for the welfare of religion that their credit
should spread until all consciences pass into their
keeping."[26]

This accusation of personal ambition is not
justified. The Jesuits were splendidly ambitious, but
not for themselves. Let us be more just to them
than Pascal, who blamed them for deserting the
lofty standard set by St Ignatius. In fact, their policy
never varied; their motto was *ad majorem Dei
gloriam*, and they tried, according to their lights, to
live up to it. According to their lights—these sometimes led them astray. They let themselves be caught
by the world. Endeavouring to bring religion
within the reach of all, they lowered it, and, in
Bossuet's phrase, put cushions under the elbows of
their penitents;[27] but their intention was not selfish.

Pascal and the Jansenists in general saw only the
seamy side; his prejudice led him to a false conclusion. Such is the power of that queen of errors,
the *petitio principii*.

A special form of question-begging is the red
herring, a trick which the Jesuits readily practise.
Hampered at one point they execute a rapid diver-

sion, and go off on a side-issue. In the seventeenth
letter Pascal presses them to state whether or no
it is true that they "permettent de tuer pour une
pomme". This is a question of fact which they
answer with the parrot cry, "the writer of these
letters is a heretic and therefore unworthy of
credence". And the evidence of his heresy and consequent untrustworthiness is an alms-box, broken
open in the church of St Merri by one of his friends,
it is alleged. To which Pascal blandly replies, "You
might open all the alms-boxes in Paris without
affecting my orthodoxy".[28] This cry of heresy is the
refrain, supplied by Annat, of all the *Première réponse*.
Annat wrote: "L'on pouvait ne donner autre réponse à ces mauvaises lettres que ces trois mots—les
Jansénistes sont hérétiques." This is at best the logic
of Tilburina.

But, it may be said, when Pascal suddenly dropped
his defence of Arnauld, and, from the fourth letter
onward to the fifteenth, turned to pillory the moral
teaching of the casuists, was he not shirking the issue,
drawing a red herring across the track, creating a
captious diversion? A moment's consideration will
shew that he was not. Having failed, for all his
eloquence and cunning fence, to save his friend, he
begins to look close at the ethics of those who had
undone him; and as he reads the books of casuistry,

Escobar and Bauny and the rest, conveying those ethics, he discovers that what is after all at stake is not the reputation and welfare of one human being, but the cause of Christian morality itself, imperilled by their vicious teaching. Shocked and alarmed he rises to defend that cause. The task, he feels, is laid upon him by Heaven.

The force, the very violence of his attack is explained by his conviction that God was on his side, approving and blessing. What induced this conviction? It was the miracle of the Holy Thorn on 24 March 1656, when he was in the thick of the fight, between the fifth and sixth letters. His little niece, Margot Périer, aged ten, "en pension" at Port-Royal de Paris, was suddenly relieved of a loathsome lacrymal ulcer by application of a relic, a thorn from Christ's crown.[29] The cure, attested by the best medical evidence, was hailed as a miracle by Port-Royal, and denounced as devilry by the Jesuits. For Pascal it was the formal and divine sanction of his warfare. He had a new seal engraved with a new device, a crown of thorns, and the motto "scio cui credidi". The wording is significant. Hitherto he had believed; now he knew. Henceforth he would not sheathe his blade till he had slain the monster and vindicated the cause of Truth and of God. As a good logician and man of science, he refuses to mix the orders. "Laissons là leurs différends," he cries at the close of the third letter, "ce sont des disputes de théologiens et non pas de théologie. Nous, qui ne sommes point docteurs, n'avons que faire à leurs démêlés". And with that he quits the quarrel of Jesuits, Jacobins, and Jansenists, and concentrates attack upon the Jesuits alone, who are responsible for the stream of poison. Viewed thus, the diversion, the change of subject, was perfectly legitimate.

Another sin against reason, logic, and clear thought is ambiguity in the use of terms—taking a word in two different senses. This is a branch of equivocation. It is so extravagant that it cannot escape the eye. For instance,

> Loss of liberty is slavery.
> I have lost the liberty of leaving my light unscreened at night,
> Therefore I am a slave.

The conclusion is faulty because "liberty" in the major is not the same as "liberty" in the minor.

Childish as this sophistry is, the Jesuits did not hesitate to use it. Saint-Cyran, the director and spiritual father of Port-Royal, having said in a letter of condolence on a domestic loss: "que le plus agréable sacrifice qu'on puisse offrir à Dieu dans ces rencontres est celui de la patience", Father Meynier, S.J., took him to task and accused him of Calvinism. Why? Because evidently he rejects "the Sacrifice of the Mass, which is the most agreeable of all to God". This is nothing more nor less than a pun, and a poor one at that. Pascal once allows himself the same licence. He closes his first letter thus: "Je vous laisse cependant dans la liberté de tenir pour le mot de prochain, ou non, car j'aime trop mon prochain pour le persécuter sous ce prétexte." It is a pun and not a bad one; it shocked his Port-Royal friends and they cut it out of the second edition.³⁰ But to return. The Jesuits were not good logicians. Blinded by anger and fear, they fall into another gross incon- sequence. When arguments fail them, they appeal to authority, to the doctrine of probable opinions. What is this? "Je vois bien", says the good Father of the fifth letter, "que vous ne savez pas ce que c'est que la doctrine des opinions probables. Vous par- leriez autrement si vous la saviez. Ah! vraiment il faut que je vous en instruise. Vous n'aurez pas perdu votre temps d'être venu ici; sans cela vous ne pouviez rien entendre. C'est le fondement et l'A.B.C. de toute notre morale." Now Probabilism (i.e. the doctrine which teaches that in case of doubt whether a thing is right or wrong, whether you are free to do it or barred by a restrictive law, you may safely follow the opinion of authorities, and even of a single authority, provided it be grave, even though your conscience tells you otherwise) was not the invention of the Jesuits. It was the gift of a Dominican, Bartolomé de Medina (1528–1581); but the Jesuits adopted it and practised it eagerly. It suited their object, viz. the glory of God by means of a great cloud of witnesses. They would lead all men at all costs to worship Him.

Now there has never been a lack of authorities, of grave doctors. The Jesuits had an ample choice, and to them they made appeal rather than engage in the arduous task of finding proofs. Thus, in order to prove that calumny of a calumniator is not a mortal sin, Father Dicastillus presents, not proofs, but a long list of other Jesuits of repute, University professors and imperial and ducal confessors, blinding the enquirer with a shower of academic and golden dust.[31]

Pascal will have none of it. The Jesuit authorities do not in the least impress him. "Est ce que le P. Bauny et Bazile Ponce ne peuvent pas rendre leur opinion probable?" asks the complaisant Father "Je ne me contente pas du probable," he answers, "je cherche le sûr."[32] He knew but one way of salvation, and that a narrow one, and this multiplication of divergent and accommodating paths per-

plexed and angered him. And of course the sub-
stitution of authority for proof is a betrayal of logic.
At the same time it must be admitted that while
Probabilism opens the door to soft decisions on the
part of the confessor and therefore to lax morality
on the part of the penitent, there are many cases in
which its use is necessary and a help in forming
conscience and directing conduct. Probabilism
cannot harm the soul which seeks help in deter-
mining what is right or wrong from the utterance
of wise teachers, hearkens to conscience in selecting
guidance, and submits all decisions to the higher, the
supreme law of God. It does harm when the variety
of opinion is used not to solve honest doubt but to
excuse continuance in sin. It was for those who thus
abused it that Pascal was fearful, and it cannot be
denied that his sharp rebuke of methods which
minister to sin was necessary and beneficial.

These moral considerations have led us away from
logic and want of logic, to which we must now get
back. When they run short of proofs, and short even
of authorities, the Jesuits resort to abuse. Controversy in the seventeenth century was not mealy-
mouthed; but the defence against the Little Letters
is vituperative to the point of Billingsgate. The
method is indeed "No case; blacken plaintiff's
attorney".

At the beginning of the twelfth letter Pascal culls a bouquet of epithets and titles, and there were more to follow: "Impie, bouffon, ignorant, farceur, imposteur, calomniateur, fourbe, hérétique, calviniste déguisé, disciple de Du Moulin, possédé d'une légion de diables." He might have added the ugliest of all, "esprit lascif", which the English translator renders "lascivious beast". Even the Abbé Maynard, their nineteenth-century champion, allows that the first replies of the Jesuits, "though substantially solid, were feeble in form and especially marred by invective".[33] Pascal, on the other hand, never offends against good taste. He behaves as a gentleman; irritable and violent by nature, he keeps himself under control. The manners and style of his opponents disgust him: "Je vous plains, mes pères, d'avoir recours à de tels remèdes."[34] His replies, for all their fierceness, never break the rules of decency. True, he is wroth, his irony breaks out into indignation, but it is the indignation of the man of the world whose common sense is outraged by futile sophistry, of the man of feeling who is moved by the persecution of the innocent, of the Christian who desires to preserve from stain the pure morality of the Gospel.

His attack is no doubt open to criticism at more than one point. Probabilism, as we have seen, is not the noxious weed he thought it. It is the necessary consequence of a system of obligatory and universal confession, for the confessor, perplexed by the multitude and variety of the sins he has to hear, is bound to consult opinion for the solution of cases which lie outside his personal experience.[35] Close scrutiny of the quotations which Pascal makes from the casuists disclose a few, surprisingly few slips. He never gives his foe the benefit of the doubt, he makes the most of every advantage, he writes as an advocate and with an advocate's bias; but there can be no question, I think, that the effect of his bitter campaign was to raise the moral tone of his time, to fortify the conscience against misuse of casuistry, and set an example of honest debate. In a word, he won a great spiritual and moral victory. He had to wait a whole generation, more than thirty years after his death, for the appearance of a foeman at all worthy of his steel. It was not till 1694 that Père Daniel, the historian,[36] took up the glove, a glove stained with the blood of his order. His *Entretiens de Cléandre et d'Eudoxe*, written by way of answer to Perrault's *Parallèles des anciens et des modernes*, with their eulogy of the *Provinciales*,[37] are indeed much superior to Jesuit efforts during Pascal's life-time, and they contain some sound remarks on the question of Probabilism; but their immediate result was to set men reading Pascal and to procure a French transla-

tion of Wendrock's (i.e. Nicole's) Latin commentary! Daniel was rash enough to venture on a
criticism of Pascal's style and grammar. His blunder-
buss missed fire. We shall see presently how and
why Pascal remains the uncontested master of
French prose. For the moment it is enough to seek
in his style the key to the art of honest debate.

It is the style of a man who, with all his faults, was
devoted to the cause of Truth and the pursuit of
Truth. Not indeed of Truth in and for itself, but as
the expression of God's will and a means of union
with Him through Love; "On se fait une idole de
la vérité même; car la vérité hors de la charité n'est
pas Dieu" (fr. 582). Yet to refuse to love the Truth
is to refuse to love God. To lie, to prevaricate and
equivocate is to commit a mortal sin against Reason[38]
which in matters of fact, outside revelation, is as the
word of God which is Truth.[39]

This love of Truth brought him one day into a
clash with his friends. In 1661 Port-Royal was faced
with a hideous dilemma. A Formulary had been put
out by authority to which signature was required of
all religious persons, confessing that the propositions
condemned by Rome were present in Jansen's
Augustinus. If the nuns signed this they betrayed
their teachers; if they declined to sign, they were
open to excommunication. The "Messieurs" had

to find a way round. First they tried a preamble, declaring submission on the point of doctrine ("question de droit") and respectful silence on the point of fact, i.e. the existence of the propositions in the book ("question de fait"). The preamble being forbidden, they tried a postscript, to the same effect. Pascal would have none of it. There must be no paltering with the Truth. The suggested reservation was abominable in the sight of God, contemptible in the eyes of men, and of no avail with enemies bent on their undoing. So he wrote in a pamphlet (*Écrit sur la signature*).[40] The "Messieurs" met in his chamber, hoping to bring him to reason. In the thick of the discussion Pascal fainted, and the company broke up. When he came to himself, his sister asked him what was the matter. To her he replied: "When I saw these men give way whom I regarded as the trustees of Truth and its proper champions, I was so distressed that I could not hold out." His sister, Jacqueline the nun, was beforehand with him and had set him an example. Confronted with the choice of schism or heresy, she rejected the proposed compromise disdainfully: "Il n'y a que la vérité qui délivre véritablement et il est sans doute qu'elle ne délivre que ceux qui la mettent en liberté en la confessant avec fidélité."[41] She had not the courage of her conviction and she signed at last; but she died of it. The brother's swoon, the sister's death are a twofold sacrifice to Truth; and it is to be noted that Blaise quotes the same text as Jacqueline (John viii. 32) in proclaiming the emancipating power of Truth.[42]

Of course the Jesuits also loved God, but they did not love Truth to this point of heroism. When occasion required they did not hesitate to depart from truth, inviting the exclamation of the Capuchin Valeriano Magni, *Mentiris impudentissime*.[43] This did not seriously damage their sacerdotal character; for it must be confessed that strict veracity, though a Christian, has not always been an ecclesiastical, virtue. The Fathers of the fourth century shew what is to us a strange indifference to exactitude in their citations and allegations, no doubt due to the rhetoric which formed the basis of their education. And the Jesuits of the seventeenth century were tarred with the same brush. We cannot really trust their word. The fact is that the world is apt to shrink from distasteful truth, and endeavouring to win the world the Jesuits came to terms with it and, like it, winked at untruth. They lacked the courage to face it, and for that courage is needed. Pascal did not love those who did not love and seek the Truth whether they were friends or foes. He could love a foe who loved Truth and embraced it bravely, but one of his

Pensées runs: "Les gens manquent du cœur: on n'en ferait pas son ami" (fr. 196). He had the rare courage to correct the errors of fact, the slips of logic into which he chanced to fall. The postscript to the sixteenth letter shews him asking pardon. He had mistakenly attributed the Jesuit answers to their ally and associate Desmarets de Saint-Sorlin. He apologizes, retracts, and invites his adversaries to follow his example.[44]

The incident of the Formulary which I have already described gives rise to another palinode. Much of the quarrel between Jansenist and Jesuit turned on the distinction between "fait" and "droit". Was it true, yes or no, that Jansen was author of the five condemned propositions? This was a question of fact. Supposing it proved that he was their author, was he wrong to have written them; *aliter*, were the propositions orthodox or heretical? This was a question of doctrine. The Jesuits declined to draw the distinction. Pascal insists upon it at length in the eighteenth letter. But the day came when the distinction he there claimed seemed to him illicit—the day when the Formulary required signature condemning the propositions as the authentic utterance of Jansen. He was now convinced that the distinction between "fait" and "droit" was impossible under the circumstances, and he rejected it vehemently in his *Écrit sur la signature*, which, as we saw, nearly brought him to a breach with his friends. He pours scorn upon himself and his fly-sheets: "Un très petit nombre de personnes, qui font à toute heure de petits écrits volants, disent que le fait est de sa nature séparé du droit."

His controversy throughout is marked by bold love of Truth and close reasoning. Taken apart, these qualities do not suffice for the conduct of honest debate. You may love the Truth, but lack the power to give effect to your love; you may reason close upon false premisses. Combine love of Truth with logic and you enter upon possession of a mighty instrument which falsehood and false logic cannot withstand. It is the sword of the giant; "And the priest said, the sword of Goliath the Philistine, behold it is here. And David said, There is none like that, give it me."

CHAPTER II

Pascal as Moralist

What is a moralist? He is one who teaches moral duty, or who remarks on moral conduct. He is not necessarily moral himself. Seneca inculcated stern morality, but he was not a strong character. Rousseau and Voltaire taught behaviour to their generation; but Dr Johnson at least found it difficult to settle the proportion of iniquity between them.[1]

Now it is possible, though not perhaps very wise, to deny that Pascal was a speculative philosopher;[2] but no one not blinded with prejudice will withhold from him the title of moralist, nor refuse to admit that he practised what he preached and profoundly influenced the ethics of his time.

The questions which this chapter has to consider are, first, what sort of morality did he preach, and secondly, what did he achieve in the sphere of moral conduct?

To take the last question first; in Sainte-Beuve's vigorous phrase, he killed the casuistry of the school-men, just as Descartes sapped their metaphysic.[3]

Casuistry, the treatment of cases of conscience, is

a harmless, necessary process; but in the hands of seventeenth-century Jesuits it became a thing against which much may be said; and Pascal said it. The *Provincial Letters* dealt a blow from which the theory and practice of Jesuit casuistry have never recovered. The terms "Jesuitry, Jesuitical" still sting, and they are the bitter fruit of Pascal's polemic.[4] That polemic was, as we saw, in one important particular, unfair. In attributing to the Jesuits the motive of personal ambition, Pascal did them signal wrong. But the general judgment, I believe, is that he was justified in accusing them of betrayal of a sacred trust. What was it then that led them astray in their handling of moral problems? Primarily it was the legal habit of mind which measures things spiritual by the canons of the law-court. But a subsidiary, subtle, and extremely potent agency was an astonishing want of taste, the sources of which are obscure but the effects of which are manifest.[5] In the first half of the seventeenth century a wave of bad taste swept over France, tainting every branch of intellectual activity; and the Society of Jesus, which might have taken as its second motto *humani nihil a me alienum puto*, did not escape the infection.

Symptoms of the disease were, in literature, burlesque, the pedestrian epic, the "préciosité" of the salon; in politics, the tragi-comedy of the Fronde;

in art, baroque extravagance of decoration such as the Jesuits used in their churches;[6] in theology, their books of easy devotion and fulsome eulogy of their own order.[7] The Classical movement of the latter half of the century was needed to stem the tide. Poussin, the first great classical painter, turned with disgust from the antics of Scarron;[8] and the mission of Pascal, standing on the threshold of the movement and through his devotion to truth its authentic herald, was to clear Christian thought and conduct from the corruption due to the supremacy of the juridical ideal and the vagaries of perverted taste.

To correct this last he spoke to men of the world, men of good taste, in terms which they understood—hence the swift success of his Letters. But in adopting their tone and attitude, in addressing men of the world as a man of the world, he produced a result which he certainly did not intend. He sealed the charter of "honnêteté", he confirmed the code of the "bien-séances", the living illustration of which was his mundane friends, Méré and Mitton, and its detailed description that supplied by La Rochefoucauld in his *Réflexions sur la Société*. "Il faudrait faire son plaisir de celui des autres, ménager leur amour-propre, et ne le blesser jamais.... Il faut contribuer, autant qu'on le peut, au divertissement des personnes avec qui on veut vivre; mais il ne faut pas être toujours chargé du soin d'y contribuer. Le commerce des honnêtes gens ne peut subsister sans une certaine sorte de confiance; elle doit être commune entre eux, il faut que chacun ait un air de sûreté et de discrétion qui ne donne jamais lieu de craindre qu'on puisse rien dire par imprudence."

"Honnêteté", as thus described, is a fine quality, and the "bien-séances" as sound a set of principles for social behaviour as can be desired. But they fall below the level of Christ's teaching and the practice of His saints. They are not real virtue, but simply the equipment of the well-bred. Pascal had been for a brief period, a year and a half, himself an "honnête homme", moving in the circle of "honnêtes gens"; and even after he had left them and betaken himself to the austere company of Port-Royal, he retained his respect for rank, its privileges and its obligations. He bids the young noble for whom he composed the *Discours sur la condition des grands* remember that "noblesse oblige", and that even if he fails to reach the height of conduct at which he ought to aim, even if he loses his soul, he must always remain "un honnête homme".

And in the *Pensées* the quality of "honnêteté" is preferred above every other distinction: "One must not say of a man, 'he is a mathematician or a preacher or eloquent, but he is a gentleman'. That universal quality alone pleases me."[9]

And to Fermat, the famous mathematician, he writes, excusing his inability to visit him at Toulouse: "Though you are in my opinion the greatest geometer in Europe, that is not the quality which would have drawn me, but the thought of the wit and 'honnêteté' which your conversation would assuredly have afforded me." By the date of this letter (1660)[10] he had said good-bye to mathematics, and was as busy as his wretched health allowed preparing his great Apology. But he could not forget the charm of polite society; and indeed it is the last thing that a man of taste is willing to forgo.

The writer "to a country friend describing the troubles in the Sorbonne" is a man of the world. The first and second letters strike the note. "Tout le monde les entend...elles sont agréables aux gens du monde"—so runs the criticism of them which he puts into the mouth of his friend.[11] All through the fiction of the adopted character there sounds the accent of Pascal's personal conviction, and as the series of the letters grows, and the theology which he at first disclaimed asserts itself and dominates the scene, the point of view persists of the honest man, outraged by offences against good taste and good

breeding, against the manners and morals of re-
spectable and self-respecting society.

By his pillorying of anti-social vices—hypocrisy,
equivocation, slander and so on—he sealed the
charter of "honnêteté".[12] That was not his principal
purpose, which was quite other. As we see from the
Pensées his hope and desire was to wean the "honnête homme" to higher things, although his advice
to the little Prince de Luynes shews that he recognized "honnêteté" as being worthy of respect.
But it belonged to the order of the flesh. Its possessor
might also stand in the order of the mind; but high
above both, and only attainable by those upon whom
God bestows Grace, is the order of charity. "The
greatest of the three is Charity", says St Paul. Pascal
refines and distinguishes further: "De tous les corps
ensemble on ne saurait en faire réussir une petite
pensée; cela est impossible et d'un autre ordre. De
tous les corps et esprits on n'en saurait tirer un
mouvement de vraie charité; cela est impossible et
d'un autre ordre, surnaturel" (fr. 793).

Pascal had passed through the two lower orders.
He was well-born. He had been from childhood
surrounded by honourable example; he had received
from his patient father an education suited to his
condition; he had learnt the rules of good behaviour,
and when he came to manhood he moved without

challenge among men of like up-bringing.[13] In virtue of his astonishing genius and his notable contributions to science he stood at the very top of the order of the mind. And by the Grace of God he entered finally into the order of charity, of saintliness. His sister's portrait of him is not a whit exaggerated: "All his powers were consecrated to the knowledge and practice of perfect Christian morality, to which he bent all the talents with which God had endowed him."[14]

What was his notion of perfect Christian morality? In contrast with the natural law of morality divinely implanted in the conscience he sets the rival human systems of Stoic and Epicurean as represented by Epictetus and Montaigne.[15] Each of these philosophers had hold of a truth—Epictetus seeing the dignity and greatness of man, Montaigne, his imbecility. One would think that a perfect morality would result from a combination of the two views. But as a fact they are mutually destructive. Each describes man in terms of nature, and natural man cannot be at once great and weak. The antinomy is solved by the Christian religion, which ascribes man's weakness to nature and his greatness to the operation of Grace. This amazing union is the work of God, and it is the image of the ineffable union of two natures in the Person of the God-man Jesus

Christ. In contrast with the corrupt morality of the day which has crept into houses of religion and the literature of piety[16] Pascal proclaims the perfect morality. He draws it from the fountain head, the Mediator, sole channel of communication with God, the great law-giver.[17] Through Him alone are right doctrine and right morality conveyed to man. But this morality is not a matter of subtle distinction and paradox like that of the Porch, nor hide-bound by syllogism and legal precedent like that of the School. Founded upon principles which are inwardly accepted, it becomes an instinct and makes light of merely intellectual morality. It is free from rule, or rather you make your own rules[18] in accordance with the broad precepts laid down by the Lord. These appeal straight to the heart; they are felt, and once felt they are a sure guide to right conduct.

Perfect Christian morality was in Pascal's eyes exemplified by his friends the Solitaries of Port-Royal, whose life of renunciation and penitence was that of Egyptian hermits or of early Christians waiting for the Lord. Their asceticism was not merely a discipline but an habitual state, the only state befitting men who must wean themselves from the world and cast aside the clinging ties of human relations.

Within a dozen years of Pascal's death Madame de

Sévigné paid a visit to the valley of Chevreuse, and she describes it and its inhabitants: "C'est un vallon affreux, tout propre à faire son salut. Ce Port-Royal est une Thébaïde; c'est le paradis; c'est un désert où toute la dévotion du christianisme s'est rangée.... Il y a cinq ou six solitaires qu'on ne connaît point, qui vivent comme les pénitents de saint Jean-Climaque. Les religieuses sont des anges sur terre. Mlle de Vertus y achève sa vie avec une résignation extrême et des douleurs inconcevables; elle ne sera pas en vie dans un mois."[19] Making allowance for her humour and point of feminine exaggeration, we may regard her description as correct. Now Pascal, though he was never of the inner circle, nor ever joined the Solitaries, and, as we saw, could affirm with truth that he was not "of Port-Royal",[20] and though until near the end of his life he kept in touch with the outer world (cf. his letter to Fermat), accepted the duty of self-mortification even to the manifest detriment of his health, a fact which caused him nothing but joy. "Je vous loue, mon Dieu," he writes, "et je vous bénirai tous les jours de ma vie de ce qu'il vous a plu me réduire dans l'incapacité de jouir des douceurs de la santé et des plaisirs du monde.... Ôtez de moi, Seigneur, la tristesse que l'amour de moi-même me pourrait donner de mes propres souffrances."[21]

His self-discipline expressed itself in a way repugnant to modern taste, but one quite in keeping with primitive piety, e.g. the monks of the desert who held it a sin to wash. He neglected the ordinary decencies of life. People were not particularly clean or hygienic in seventeenth-century France, but Pascal's slovenliness shocked even his sister the nun: "On m'a congratulée pour la grande ferveur qui vous élève si fort au-dessus de toutes les manières communes que vous mettez les balais au rang des meubles superflus."[22]

Even less comprehensible to us is the belt with spikes which he drove into his side with his elbow whenever temptation assailed him. No doubt it was from a laudable desire to remind himself of his human frailty; but it was extravagant. Pascal, however, was extravagant in his thoughts and acts.

Perhaps most repellent of all is his attitude towards the tender human affections. This disturbed his married sister as much as the accumulated dust of his chamber had vexed the nun, and she attempts an elaborate explanation: "He could not bear to see my children kiss me, and he said that I ought to stop them; that it could only do them harm; and that there were many other ways of shewing them affection...." When Jacqueline of Port-Royal died, he refused and repressed any expression of grief.

"Thus he shewed that he avoided the bonds of family affection; for, had he been able to cultivate them, it would certainly have been in respect of my sister whom he loved better than any one in the world. But he went still further, for not only would he not be bound to others; he would not at any price have others bind themselves to him. I am not speaking of criminal and dangerous attachments—they are low, as every one admits; I speak of the most harmless affection: and this was a matter upon which he kept the most strict watch upon himself, so as not to give rise to it, and even to prevent it; and as I did not know this, I was greatly surprised by the rebuffs I sometimes suffered, and so I said to my sister, complaining that my brother did not love me, that I seemed to vex him, even when I was tendering the most loving care in his infirmities. Upon this she told me I was wrong, that on the contrary she knew that he had for me an affection as deep as I could desire. In this way she sought to cheer me up, and I soon had proof of it; for whenever an occasion arose when I needed my brother's help he seized it with such zeal and tokens of affection that I could not doubt his great love for me; so that I attributed to his sick state the coldness with which he met the careful service by which I tried to ease him; the riddle was only explained to me the day of his death, when a person of the most exalted gifts and piety with whom he had deeply discussed the practice of virtue told me that among other lessons he had taught him this, never to allow anyone to attach himself to him in love; that it was a fault to which we pay too little attention, because we do not recognize its greatness, nor consider that in fostering and allowing these attachments, we engage the heart, and as that should belong to God alone, it was robbing Him of His most precious possession."[23]

This account is confirmed by a *Pensée*: "It is wrong that men should bind themselves to me, even though they do so with pleasure and of their free will. I should deceive those in whom I had created this desire, for I am not the last end of any one and have not the means to satisfy them...they ought not to attach themselves to me; for they ought to spend their life and their care in pleasing God or seeking Him" (fr. 471).

This explanation—we can hardly call it justification—of his attitude is lofty in conception and consonant with St Augustine's warning not to dwell in earthly things.[24] Indeed it is a practical application of the paradoxical words of Christ: "He that hateth not his father and his mother is not worthy of me." The hyperbole appealed to Pascal's all-consuming zeal for the Lord.

I have dwelt at length upon Pascal and his family, for it discloses one of the strangest characteristics of this strange being.

All this is undoubtedly narrow, and it must be admitted that Pascal's view of human duty was narrow. It is the narrowness of the Jansenist creed, which through the mouth of its prophet Saint-Cyran proclaimed that the Christian life should be one of perpetual penitence, and that the sin of Adam is still a running sore, even despite the salutary effect of baptism.[25] It is the narrowness of the morbid mind that saw in man "naught but disguise, falsehood and hypocrisy, both in himself and in regard to others" (fr. 100 *ad fin.*). But it is the narrowness of one who after distractions of varying kind and force, perhaps in the very midst of them, despite temptation to follow the broad and easy path of "honnêteté", set his feet in the strait way to which his reading of the Gospel pointed him, and into which he strove to bring others with all the strength of his marvellous intelligence and tremendous will. It is the narrowness of one whose whole energy of love, and it was mighty, centred on one object, the Person of the Saviour, a greater than any earthly friend, whose claims are met by the cry of complete surrender: "Seigneur, je vous donne tout."[26]

Such self-consecration, if it left little room for the

play of earthly affection, left still less for indulgence
in aesthetic pleasure, and whether by temper or
training Pascal shews himself lamentably deficient
in sensibility to the beauties of nature or art. We
know that he was awestruck by the magnificence of
the starry heavens, the marvels disclosed by telescope
and microscope; but things of earth, except in so far
as they afford illustration of the disproportion of
humanity, make no appeal to him, and he was too
good a Cartesian to pay attention to brute beasts—
mere mechanical contrivances. We gather that he
had no comprehension of art. His remarks on
painting are mere commonplace and exhibit a signal
ignorance of its real purpose. He thinks only of the
likeness, the verisimilitude of a portrait, and not at
all of the essential qualities of design, composition
and colour.[27] But he had watched painters at work
and noted how they stand back from their easel in
order to criticize and correct.[28]

Of his literary sense and mastery of language I shall
speak at length later, and here will only note that
though his Puritanism condemned the stage, he had
been to the play and seen the Italian mountebanks,
and that he was familiar with the great romances of
the time.[29]

Thus there were large ranges of human interest
and activity in which he was unwilling or unable to

engage. But his application of his knowledge of man's heart and motives gives him a just claim to a high place among moral teachers, and to a hearing on various problems which strictly belong to the sciences of psychology and sociology, but always fall to be considered in their moral bearing. For example, the psychological question concerning the way in which moral principles are apprehended—the question of Conscience; the question of the effect of moral principles upon conduct—the question of Duty and Virtue; the question of the motives which lead to action or procure certitude—the question of Reason *versus* Intuition; the question of the relation of pleasure to desire—the question of Hedonism and of the *summum bonum*; the question of the relation between freedom of choice and essential freedom of will—the vexed question of Free Will and Determinism; the question of the connexion between moral ideas and practical conditions—the question of sociology, behaviour towards institutions, etc.—on each of these Pascal makes his contribution, often unexpected, always profound.

Conscience. We have already seen in chapter I how he deals with Probabilism, i.e. the notion that a thing may be safely done where there is a plausible reason —the opinion of grave authority. This was abhorrent to him. "Je ne me contente pas du probable," he cries in Letter v, "je cherche le sûr"; and in a *Pensée*: "Est-il probable que la probabilité assure? Rien ne donne l'assurance que la vérité; rien ne donne le repos que la recherche sincère de la vérité" (fr. 908), clinching his assertion with the pungent comment: "Jamais on ne fait le mal si pleinement et si gaiement que quand on le fait par conscience" (fr. 895).

Virtue. The only virtue which he recognizes is that of Jesus Christ. It is without qualification: "In Him is all our virtue and all our happiness. Apart from Him is naught but vice, misery, error, darkness, death, despair" (fr. 546). Virtue, such as man conceives it, is not only vanity but a will-o'-the-wisp that leads him farther and farther from the truth; the more sedulously it is pursued the deeper does it plunge him in error. Extreme virtue of one sort destroys the balance and blunts the effect of human effort; it invites the invasion of contrary or complementary vices: "Je n'admire point l'excès d'une vertu, comme de la valeur, si je ne vois pas en même temps l'excès de la vertu opposée...autrement ce n'est pas monter, c'est tomber" (fr. 353). "Ce que peut la vertu d'un homme ne se doit pas mesurer par ses efforts, mais par son ordinaire" (fr. 352).

Reason versus Intuition as the motive to action and the source of certitude. Here we have one of the most instructive features of Pascal's philosophy and the most open to debate, for upon the interpretation of it depends his liability to the charge of Fideism. Fideism, *aliter* Traditionalism, is the denial that natural Reason, unaided by Grace, can reach certain knowledge of primary verities, such as the existence of God, the immortality of the soul, the distinction between good and evil, etc. This is a formal heresy (though one of recent definition), being condemned by two Encyclicals of Gregory XVI (1832 and 1834), and by a canon of the Vatican Council, recalled in our own day by Pius X in his ban upon Modernism in the Bull "Pascendi dominici gregis", 1907. Its principal or most conspicuous adherents are the Abbé Bautain and Lamennais. The opposite error, of which Ramon Lull, the *doctor illuminatus* of the thirteenth century, was accused but never convicted, is that man can possess the truths of Faith (as distinguished from primary truths) through the sole exercise of Reason.

Now there are passages in the *Pensées* which look like Fideism, and recent writers have freely charged Pascal with it.[30] But a moment's reflexion, not to mention a patient study of his writings, empty the accusation of all reality. Fideism has its roots in agnosticism, which denies man's power to attain certainty in any thing. It was once the fashion, set by Victor Cousin, to regard Pascal as a despairing

sceptic, but no sensible critic holds that view to-day.[31]
Pascal constantly uses sceptical expressions and arguments, but that is because he stands in the shoes of
the sceptical interlocutor whom he is seeking to
convince. He was no sceptic, *ergo* no Fideist, and the
very fact of his undertaking a defence of Christian
truth shows that he looked upon it as capable of
demonstration.

And against passages which have a sceptical and
fideistic flavour, e.g. "Le pyrrhonisme est le vrai"
(fr. 432), "Se moquer de la philosophie, c'est
vraiment philosopher" (fr. 4), "Humiliez-vous,
raison impuissante; taisez-vous, nature imbécile"
(fr. 434), must be set many others of contrary
character: "Deux excès: exclure la raison, n'ad-
mettre que la raison" (fr. 253), "La foi dit bien ce
que les sens ne disent pas, mais non pas le contraire
de ce qu'ils voient. Elle est au-dessus, et non pas
contre" (fr. 265), "Nous avons une impuissance de
prouver, invincible à tout le dogmatisme. Nous
avons une idée de la vérité, invincible à tout le
pyrrhonisme" (fr. 395).

What are the means whereby man acquires belief?
Pascal replies: "Il y a trois moyens de croire: la
raison, la coutume, l'inspiration" (fr. 245). Proofs,
recognizable and recognized by reason—historical,
exegetical—confirmed by custom—we are machines

as much as minds—these are the instruments which work upon the intellect; but full faith needs the answer of the heart and the call to that comes from God. Here is neither Fideism nor Scepticism but Christian common sense.

"Hearken to the voice of reason, not of others, but your own, if you would believe" (fr. 260). Is that Fideism?

"I would not have you submit your belief in Me [Wisdom, i.e. the Almighty, addresses mankind] without reason. I do not want to tyrannize over you....I mean to make you see clearly, by convincing proofs, signs of divinity in Me which may convince you of what I am, and establish My rule by marvels and proofs which you cannot reject, so that you may then believe the things I teach you, finding no ground for refusing them save your own ignorance whether they be true or not."[32]

"God, whose property is to govern all things with lovingkindness, puts religion into the mind by reason, and into the heart by Grace. To force it into mind and heart by violence and threats is to put not religion there but fear, *terrorem potius quam religionem.*"[33]

This last utterance is not only anti-Fideistic, but anti-Jansenist.

Hedonism. The search for happiness is a natural

instinct: "All men seek happiness.... It is the motive of all human action, even of those on the point of hanging themselves." But all are doomed to disappointment. "All complain, kings and subjects, nobles and commoners, old and young, strong and weak, learned and ignorant, sound and sick, of every land, of every time, of every age and condition."[34]

"We cannot but desire happiness and truth, but we are incapable of either."[35] Incapable because ignorant, we and our teachers the philosophers with their 288 varieties of good, not one of them genuine. All alike miss the truth of human nature, only attain a fraction of truth. For either they are bemused by the sight of man's undoubted greatness (the Stoics), or they have only eyes for his undoubted misery (the Epicureans). In other words, they do not know man.[36] Pascal supplies the answer to the riddle, a simple one. It is the Fall and its fatal consequences.

Man retains a vague, helpless sense of lost happiness, trace of a true first nature. What he has now is a second, vastly inferior nature,[37] of concupiscence, i.e. the tendency now that heaven is withdrawn to seek pleasure in things of earth, of the flesh—"the lust of the flesh, the lust of the eyes, and the pride of life".[38]

It is selfish, it is *amour-propre*; it alienates from God,

although Pascal admits that from it good rules of policy, morality, and justice have been extracted.[39] But it is a rotten thing and its fruit is rottenness. Pascal reaches the height of extravagance in describing the effects of *amour-propre*; the sour wine of the Preacher has gone to his head: "*Ecclesiastes* shows that man without God is in total ignorance and inevitable misery. For it is wretched to have the will but not the power. He would be happy and sure of *some* truth; yet he can neither know, nor desire not to know. He cannot even doubt."[40] And so "Man is naught but sham, falsehood, and hypocrisy, both in himself and in regard to others".[41]

Free Will. The story of the Fall involves the problem of Free Will. Orthodox catholicism holds that man's will, albeit enfeebled and corrupted, was by no means extinguished by the Fall. *Liberum arbitrium minime extinctum...viribus licet attenuatum et inclinatum*, so runs the finding of the Council of Trent.[42]

For Jansen, as for the Reformers, man since the Fall can will only evil, is incapable of good. His freedom is restricted to the ordinary acts of life, to a choice between this occupation or that. His will is totally ruined. He is a prey to *concupiscentia*. This in English ears has an ugly sound; still more ugly is the rendering of St John's ἐπιθυμία in our Authorized

Version—"lust". What it really means is the tendency to obey the natural impulses, uncontrolled by reason or the better nature.

Pascal, like every other orthodox catholic, accepts the thesis of the corruption, the deterioration (*inclinatio*) of man's will. His note for the first part of his Apology admits "Que la nature est corrompue. Par la nature même" (fr. 60). And he confesses: "Pour moi j'avoue qu'aussitôt que la religion chrétienne découvre ce principe que la nature des hommes est corrompue et déchue de Dieu, cela ouvre les yeux à voir partout le caractère de cette vérité; car la nature est telle qu'elle marque partout un Dieu perdu, et dans l'homme et hors de l'homme, et une nature corrompue" (fr. 441). It is of general and compelling significance, a light in the darkness, a flash revealing the whole landscape. But, accepting the fact of man's corruption (and who can deny it? or at least his glaring imperfection), Pascal does not insist on its totality. Concupiscence drags down— "porte à la terre"—[43]but it does not utterly destroy. As we saw just now, he uses terrible words to describe the effects of "amour propre", which is the true source of the original sin, self-exalted to be a final end. But he does not ascribe to it all the consequences discovered there by Jansen. Self-love is indeed powerless against our sentiment of essential greatness; our intuition—"le cœur"—provides a way of escape.

With regard to the doctrine of Predestination, which is the complement or opposite of Free Will, the Jansenists, and Pascal with them, drew back from the terrifying conclusion to which Calvin pressed the logic of St Augustine; although the view that God, by withholding from the mass of men the grace of perseverance, leaves them to welter in their vice, is not far removed from the Reformer's doctrine of damnation. But the terms "réprouvés", "damnés" are of very rare occurrence in the *Pensées*, and the *Écrits sur la Grâce* contain the categoric statement, "le salut provient de la volonté de Dieu, et la damnation de la volonté des hommes" (*Œuvres*, t. xi, p. 138). No man is lost save by his own fault and of his own will, which will is free, though God remains the absolute master.

Pascal's anxious endeavour to preserve man's freedom of will is seen in these unfinished *Écrits sur la Grâce*, which develop hints dropped in the eighteenth *Provinciale* and bring the writer almost within the Thomist camp. They cannot be described as conclusive or satisfactory. They have a scholastic tone which does not ring quite true. Compromise, the "habit de deux paroisses", is a garment which one does not expect to sit well on the somewhat angular shoulders of the stiff fighter of the *Pro-vinciales*. But Pascal was as firmly convinced as any pre-Socratic of the theory of contraries, of the fusion of opposites in the mean,[44] and for him, while ultimate truth is one and indivisible, it is the resultant of contrary truths, and heresy consists in adopting one of these to the exclusion of the rest.[45] Bent on the discovery of the one truth, he brings all his scientific method and powerful dialectic to bear upon the problem. But the relations of human freedom to divine omnipotence offer greater difficulties than any geometrical riddle; here is a knot less easy to untie than the area of the cycloid or the properties of the arithmetical triangle. Yet the fact that he did seek a middle way, that he resented the harshness of Arnauld's theology and was attracted by Nicole's efforts[46] to soften it, is of high importance in judging his moral attitude. It reveals an un-expected strain of gentleness in a man of whom a gardener at Port-Royal once said: "M. Pascal always looked as if he was just going to swear."[47]

We come to the last of the questions of which I said that though strictly speaking they belong to the sphere of psychology or sociology, they have a moral connotation—in this case less marked than in the others.

Pascal's *social creed* was simple and almost con-

ventional. He accepts without demur the present
social system. He admits the existence, and the right
to exist, of "les grands". They belong to a recognized
and legitimate order, the order of the flesh. The
Three discourses on the condition of the great which the
piety of Pierre Nicole has preserved for us and in
which we hear the voice of Pascal, if not his actual
words, assign to the great their proper place in the
world. They are rulers and they have subjects under
them; they are on a small scale fellows of the greatest
monarchs upon earth. But they and these, and those
who do them homage, are, in Biblical phrase, all
"children of concupiscence".[48]

For the highest human dignity, the king, Pascal
had, his sister says, the respect which his divine right
demands, and his behaviour during the Fronde declares his loyalty.[49] But his "pensée de derrière la
tête" taught him the true source of royal power,
"founded on the reason and the folly of the people,
and especially on their folly".[50] He is quite aware
that the king is a human being who needs distraction
as much as, nay more than, the rest, to keep him from
the misery of vacancy.[51] Yet Pascal is no democrat.
He has a Shakespearean contempt for the crowd.
"Le peuple" has some sound instincts, but on the
whole it is vain and foolish.[52] And in his analysis of
authority and law he follows the lead of Montaigne

—and in a last resort of Hobbes—in ascribing it to the caprice of custom, the chance of climate and geographical accident.[53]

Intensely individualistic as he was in his personal religion, Pascal felt deeply and declared openly the duty of Christians one to another as members of the Body of Christ. In a series of remarkable fragments, he "christianizes", as St Paul does, the Stoical conception of mankind, not as a mere bundle of human beings, but as a living organism each of whose parts is not just a part, but a thinking member.[54] Epictetus and Seneca and Marcus Aurelius insist on the duty of reciprocal service of members within the body. "Membra sumus magni corporis", says Seneca. And this duty springs from love.[55] The likeness to Gospel teaching is obvious. But the great difference between Stoicism and Christianity, in their altruism and enthusiasm for humanity, lies in the devotion which the latter pays to a personal Christ, a divine person, and in the zeal which His example inspires. Of that devotion, of that zeal, there are few more poignant expressions than the *Mystère de Jésus*, that meditation on the Passion in which Pascal pleads with the Lord and He replies with words of eternal life and present help.

The *Mystère* is no doubt self-centred, but the self-interest of the redeemed individual is merged in love for the other members and care for their common interest. The body is one, though the members are many, and the Unity which this implies and demands is realized only in the Church of which the head under Christ is the Pope. He is once at least definitely anti-Gallican: "Il n'y a presque plus que la France où il soit permis de dire que le concile est au-dessus du Pape." To his friends the Roannez he writes: "Le corps n'est non plus vivant sans le chef que le chef sans le corps. Quiconque se sépare de l'un ou de l'autre n'est plus du corps, et n'appartient plus à Jésus-Christ." A few months later, in the seventeenth *Provinciale*, he affirms: "Je n'ai d'attache sur la terre qu'à la seule église catholique, apostolique et romaine, dans laquelle je veux vivre et mourir, et dans la communion avec le Pape, son souverain chef."

Conflict between this absolute loyalty to the Pope as head of the Church and loyalty to conscience and what he deemed to be truth drew from him the defiant words: "Ad tuum, Domine Jesu, tribunal, appello", and brought him near to a breach with his friends and to the authority to which he professed sincere obedience. But loyalty to Rome prevailed at the last and he died her humble and submissive son.[56]

CHAPTER III

Pascal as Poet

What, after all, is the cause of Pascal's popularity? Why do men turn and return to him and find in him their satisfaction and delight? What, in a word, is the secret of his strength? There is hardly any limit to the width of variety of his appeal. The physicist recalls the experiments on the *Vide*; the mathematician, the mystical hexagram and the solution of the problem of the cycloid; the moralist, the logician, the lover of clear thought, rejoice in the *Lettres Provinciales*; the pious refresh their faith through the practice of the *Pensées*. But hundreds who make no claim to belong to any of these classes, or who are drawn to him in virtue of some special quality, remain under his spell for another reason. And that reason is his style, his incomparable style. Others have solved questions of science or conscience with equal skill, have argued as close, have defended the cause of morality and religion with equal learning and conviction; it is hardly too much to say that no man has written with more magic and mastery of phrase. And this triumph is more than merely

verbal; it is the triumph of a personality: "Le style
c'est l'homme." Of no one is this more true than of
Pascal. It is a true style, the style of a man impatient,
intolerant, violent, but dedicated above all else to the
pursuit of truth. "Il a toujours eu une netteté
admirable pour discerner le faux", writes his sister,
"et on peut dire que toujours et en toute chose la
vérité a été le seul objet de son esprit." We can
accept this judgment, making all allowance for
family prejudice, and despite the angry comment of
the Jesuit, the friend of Bourdaloue, "Pascal est beau
autant que le faux le peut être".[1] A passionate
sincerity is stamped on everything he wrote; and if
his passion sometimes blinded him, his sincerity, as
we have seen, led him to apologize for his mistake
when it was brought home to him.[2]

This passionate sincerity is the source of extra-
ordinary beauty of expression and originality, for
which Pascal deserves to be saluted as the inventor
and founder of modern French prose. We recognize
this brilliance to-day, but his own friends were not
so fully aware of it. If he was for them "le grand
M. Pascal", it was chiefly on account of his scientific
prowess. Greatness as a writer belonged, for them,
rather to Antoine Arnauld. The boldness which we
admire in Pascal frightened them; they ventured to
lay hands upon his language, softening and polishing

it both in the *Provinciales* and in the *Pensées*.[3] He was
indeed for them not comparable as writer with their
leader. Even the faithful Nicole, at once Pascal's
master and disciple, who paid him the highest compliment of all in an attempt to imitate him, makes
certain reserves, and takes back with one hand the
praise which he bestows with the other.[4] Mme de
Sévigné, ardent admirer of Pascal as she was, nowhere extols his "harmony" as she does that of
Arnauld; she puts him no higher than Nicole, for
whom she has an enthusiasm so extravagant that her
son Charles rebukes her for it.[5] We have no difficulty
in agreeing with Charles or with Racine, who points
a contemptuous comparison between the letters of
Nicole and those of Pascal;[6] or with Boileau, who
sets him high above all others, ancient and modern;[7]
or with the great historian Le Nain de Tillemont,
who pays him the signal, nay, for a Port-Royalist,
the almost incredible compliment, of a comparison
with St Augustine.[8]

Such was the judgment of the élite, but the general
taste of the century was less sure. It was natural that
the enemies of Port-Royal could see no merit in the
Little Letters; on the other hand even they admitted
that in Arnauld's *Fréquente Communion* exquisite
flowers of eloquence mask the poison of the treatise.[9]
Indeed, for the general, that frigid work and Nicole's

apologetic effort of the *Imaginaires et Visionnaires*
were masterpieces; and when Pierre Bayle declared
Nicole to be "une des plus belles plumes de
l'Europe" he was probably expressing the common
opinion of the century.

It will be as well at this point to consider more
closely the prose writers who were most in vogue at
the moment when Pascal began to ply his pen; and
what was the style which they respectively affected.

To begin with, there was Guez de Balzac, who
until his death in 1653 and beyond it (his *Socrate
chrétien* appeared in 1652, *Aristippe*, his favourite, in
1657 and his collected works in 1662) was venerated
and copied as the unquestioned master. As taste
improved and the educated public began to weary
of "pointes" and bombast, his reputation fell, but
his example as builder of the lofty phrase and mani-
pulator of words and cadences was held up to
admiration by such judges as La Mothe Le Vayer,
Bossuet, Boileau, Bouhours, and Saint-Évremond.[10]
Pascal laughs at him and his school, but he sometimes takes a hint from him.[11]

There was Descartes, who may be said to have
founded the prose of philosophy and science; but he
disliked writing, had little care for art or ornament,
and simply sought to give clear expression to
thought.

There were the men of Port-Royal, Robert
d'Andilly and Antoine Le Maître, who despite the
warning of their master, Saint-Cyran, "that de-
fenders of the Truth must not let their vocabulary
vex them",[12] paid close attention to literary detail
(the women, La Mère Angélique, La Mère Agnès,
and Jacqueline Pascal, were less particular), with the
result that "ces messieurs" were generally regarded
as models of style; and in particular Antoine Arnauld
and Pierre Nicole, already mentioned, of whom we
may say, the dust of ancient controversy having
settled, that Arnauld for all his vigour and learning
lacked grace while Nicole was more at home in
Latin than in French, wherein as we saw he tried to
follow Pascal, and may therefore be left out of the
account. We may look at Arnauld and Descartes side
by side with Pascal in passages more or less *in pari
materia*.

Intellectual Experience

DESCARTES

Mais je ne craindrai pas de dire
que je pense avoir eu beaucoup
d'heur de m'être rencontré dès
ma jeunesse en certains chemins
qui m'ont conduit à des con-
sidérations et des maximes dont
j'ai formé une méthode par
laquelle il me semble que j'ai
moyen d'augmenter par degrés

PASCAL

J'avais passé longtemps dans
l'étude des sciences abstraites; et
le peu de communication qu'on
en peut avoir m'en avait dé-
goûté. Quand j'ai commencé
l'étude de l'homme, j'ai vu que
ces sciences abstraites ne sont pas
propres à l'homme, et que je
m'égarais plus de ma condition

ma connaissance, et de l'élever peu à peu au plus haut point auquel la médiocrité de mon esprit et la courte durée de ma vie lui pourront permettre d'atteindre. Car j'en ai déjà recueilli de tels fruits qu'encore au jugement que je fais de moi-même je tâche toujours de pencher vers le côté de la défiance plutôt que vers celui de la présomption, et que, regardant d'un œil de philosophe les diverses actions et entreprises de tous les hommes, il n'y en ait quasi aucune qui ne me semble vaine et inutile, je ne laisse pas de recevoir une extrême satisfaction du progrès que je pense avoir déjà fait en la recherche de la vérité, et de concevoir de telles espérances pour l'avenir que si, entre les occupations des hommes, purement hommes, il y en a quelqu'une qui soit solidement bonne et importante, j'ose croire que c'est celle que j'ai choisie.

Discours de la Méthode, 1.

en y pénétrant que les autres en les ignorant. J'ai pardonné aux autres d'y peu savoir. Mais j'ai cru trouver au moins bien des compagnons en l'étude de l'homme, et que c'est la vraie étude qui lui est propre. J'ai été trompé; il y en a encore moins qui l'étudient que la géométrie. Ce n'est que manque de savoir étudier cela qu'on cherche le reste; mais n'est-ce pas que ce n'est pas encore là la science que l'homme doit avoir, et qu'il lui est meilleur de s'ignorer pour être heureux?

Pensées, fr. 144.

Spiritual Healing

ARNAULD

Lorsqu'un malade peut souffrir les incisions et les remèdes les plus violents il n'est pas besoin

PASCAL

Il y a différents degrés dans cette aversion pour la vérité; mais on peut dire qu'elle est dans tous d'une si parfaite connaissance pour le guérir, mais lorsqu'il est réduit dans un tel état et dans une telle faiblesse qu'il ne peut souffrir ni les maux ni les remèdes, un médecin a besoin d'une suffisance et d'une sagesse extraordinaire pour savoir dans toute l'étendue de son art jusqu'où la condescendance raisonnable peut aller; pour s'éloigner également ou d'une douceur cruelle ou d'une indiscrète sévérité; et pour combattre tellement la maladie qu'il n'affaiblisse trop le malade. Comme donc la connaissance de cet art est d'autant plus nécessaire aux médecins de la terre pour la guérison des corps que les malades sont moins disposés à prendre les remèdes, aussi la connaissance de la vérité est d'autant plus nécessaire au médecin du ciel pour la guérison des âmes que les pénitents sont moins disposés à faire pénitence; parce que c'est à lui à soutenir souvent la faiblesse qu'il trouve en eux par la force et la bonne disposition du fond du cœur, et à rendre utiles les moindres actions de ceux qu'il conduit par le mouvement de la piété solide dans laquelle il doit tâcher de l'établir.

La Fréquente Communion
(1643), Préface, pp. 39 ff.

en quelque degré, parce qu'elle est inséparable de l'amour propre. C'est cette mauvaise délicatesse qui oblige ceux qui sont dans la nécessité de reprendre les autres, de choisir tant de détours et de tempéraments pour éviter de les choquer. Il faut qu'ils diminuent nos défauts, qu'ils fassent semblant de les excuser, qu'ils y mêlent des louanges et des témoignages d'affection et d'estime. Avec tout cela, cette médecine ne laisse pas d'être amère à l'amour-propre. Il en prend le moins qu'il peut, et toujours avec dégoût et souvent même avec un secret dépit contre ceux qui la lui présentent. Il arrive de là que, si on a quelque intérêt d'être aimé de nous, on s'éloigne de nous rendre un office qu'on sait nous être désagréable; on nous traite comme nous voulons être traités; nous haïssons la vérité, on nous la cache; nous voulons être flattés, on nous flatte; nous aimons à être trompés, on nous trompe.

Pensées, fr. 100.

Pascal's style as exhibited in these passages is concise, and the expression of deep thought is extremely simple. But it is not in dimension or depth that the difference lies between him and Descartes and Arnauld. They wield an elaborate and highly complicated phrase, full of parentheses and charged with subordinate clauses. But so does Pascal upon occasion. Father Daniel, the Jesuit historian, writing a whole generation later, when the reign of the grammarian and of the votary of conciseness was established, reproaches him, not without cause, for his incorrectness of speech, the redundancy of his relative pronouns and conjunctions, his "quis" and "ques".[13] The difference is not here. The fact is that the prose of Descartes and Arnauld, for all its dignity, is lit with a cold light; that of Pascal is shot through with warmth and passion which renders it "quick and powerful".

A homely simile may perhaps be permitted. At Vichy or Bath, or wherever suffering humanity seeks a cure, there is a long soak in the deep pool, comforting but dull. Then into the still water air is pumped—oxygen or carbonic acid—and the radio-active liquid boils and bubbles like a live thing and becomes a tonic as well as a relief. Such, in contrast with the best prose of his day, is the prose of Pascal. The marvellous results which he obtains are largely due to the skill with which he varies the expression of his thought according to the requirements of his topic. The *Provinciales* provide instances of this on every page; but it is the *Pensées* which exhibit the art of Pascal at its highest point. I say deliberately "his art", for it is a mistake to say, as is sometimes said, that in the *Pensées* thought and expression are one and definitive, that he flashes his thought upon you immediately, in its final form, without reflection, in a single inspiration.[14] A remark by his sister, Mme Périer, in the Life of her brother does indeed lend itself to this belief: "Il était maître de son style; en sorte que non seulement il disait tout ce qu'il voulait, mais il le disait en la manière qu'il voulait, et son discours faisait l'effet qu'il s'était proposé."[15] But this was not found without effort. The Letters were doubtless sometimes composed at white heat, e.g. the first, with its air of a man of the world who does not trouble himself over grammatical nicety. Others were the fruit of much labour and revision. The thirteenth was rewritten seven or eight times.

Certainly some *Pensées* are swift and apparently unpremeditated; but others bear traces of a most careful and laborious confection. Let us watch him at work, and for this purpose turn to the great passage on the two infinites between which man is set (fr. 72).

Though it lacks the heading "A.P.R." or "demain" which accompanies certain *Pensées* and obviously refers to the lecture he was about to deliver to the assembled Messieurs on that June afternoon in 1658,[16] when he unfolded the plan of his Apology, this piece is probably intended for that; the writer is on his mettle and sets about the work with due deliberation and care.

He takes a folio quire of fine paper (37 cm.×22½) and he covers eight pages with elegant penmanship, in spite of a rapidity which forbids the full formation of every letter (the "ment" of "intelligiblement" fades into "m—"). The lines are regular and well spaced. He has his Montaigne in hand or in his head, for he has his eye all the time on the free-thinking for whom the *Essais* were a breviary, and he starts from the descriptions of Nature in I 25, and II 12.

The first runs thus: "Qui se présente comme dans un tableau cette grande image de notre mère Nature en son entière majesté; qui lit en son visage une si générale et constante variété; qui se remarque là-dedans, et non soi, mais un royaume, comme un trait d'une pointe très délicate, celui-là estime les choses selon leur juste valeur. Ce grand monde, que les uns multiplient encore comme espèces sous un genre, c'est le miroir où il nous faut regarder pour nous connaître de bon biais."

The second: "Qui lui a persuadé que le branle admirable de la voûte céleste, la lumière éternelle de ces flambeaux roulant si fièrement sur sa tête. . . soient établis. . . pour sa commodité et pour son service?"

Here is matter for Pascal's purpose, which is Montaigne's and something more. Montaigne, the amused, indulgent observer, allows man's incapacity to know nature; Pascal accepts this, adds the reason, and points a moral lesson. "Incapacité de l'homme", the heading of fr. 72, is replaced by "Disproportion de l'homme". Man is out of proportion with the universe; there is no real basis of comparison. Nature is infinite, infinitely great and infinitely little. Man is finite and limited. The thought is humiliating but wholesome, for it bids him seek an explanation elsewhere. Humiliating, for if our knowledge of nature is not true, there is no truth available; and if it is true, there is no room for boasting. Man, either way, is humbled to the dust. Yet man cannot live without seeking knowledge; before we embark on a deep enquiry into nature let us look closely and boldly at ourselves, and recognize our want of proportion with her. *Aliter*, either our impressions of nature are all wrong, or, if right, they shew that truth is out of reach. That is Pascal's first draft; but it displeases him; it begs the question. He strikes it out with three vigorous vertical strokes and begins again, this time working Montaigne into the body of his text and adapting him as he goes.

The words which catch his imagination and which he would retain are "entière majesté" and "pointe très délicate" from the first passage; and "lumière éternelle de ces flambeaux roulant si fièrement..." from the second. Montaigne's splendid phrase describes the movement of the planets. Pascal particularizes. He brings the sun into the place of honour. He is not yet a convinced Copernican, "Je trouve bon qu'on n'approfondisse pas l'opinion de Copernic" (fr. 218), but the "greater light", the most notable of nature's phenomena, supplies an impressive and surprising contrast. Its vast orbit is but a tiny speck compared with that of the glittering host. So he turns his eye upward and away from man and his habitation (Montaigne's "soi", "tout un royaume", which are after all only "des objets bas qui l'environnent").

It is only after repeated experiments that his sentence, bristling with recollections of Montaigne, issues in its final form. He prunes and simplifies, eschewing unnecessary words. "Des immensités de l'espace" disappears after "concevoir" and "en" before "fournir", and we are left with two absolute verbs, which gives incomparable terseness and force: "Elle se lassera plutôt de concevoir que la Nature de fournir". The concrete replaces the abstract; "l'am-plitude" becomes "l'ample sein de la Nature"; "point" becomes "pointe". He avoids the jingle "considère...entière", substituting "contemple". He heaps up expressions to mark the contrast between man and nature, nature and the sum of things, the universe of infinity. Man is lost in a forgotten corner of nature, the universe itself is but a wretched little dungeon. What then is a man in presence of Infinity? "Qu'est-ce qu'un homme devant l'Infini?" Pre-sently he will reduce the scale in one direction and increase it in another, and cry "Qu'est-ce que *l'homme* dans la Nature?" but not until he has completed the picture by exhibiting the other extreme, the in-finitely little. For this he borrows from scientific accounts of the wonders revealed by the microscope, then in process of development, either Hobbes, *De corpore*, c. xxxviii, 1, or perhaps rather Pierre Borel, whose *Centuria observationum microscopicarum* had appeared at The Hague in 1656. Borel expatiates on the atom, the tininess of insects, the veins and articulations of the fly, and even the figures of stars found in leaves, quite in the manner of the passage with which we are engaged.[17]

It is easy to smile, with Havet,[18] at Pascal's zoology and cosmology, his universes concentrated in a mite; but popular science to-day takes a more serious view.

Sir James Jeans, in his *Mysterious Universe*, has the following passage: "The carbon atoms... consist of six electrons revolving round the appropriate nucleus like six planets revolving round a central sun." Here is at least a striking analogy.

On the other hand, the same writer suggests a curious contrast between the effect produced upon the modern mind by the revelations of the telescope and the amazement and awe of the seventeenth-century astronomer, gazing into the depths of the sky. "Il tremblera dans la vue de ces merveilles", says Pascal; and Jeans, "It is probably unnecessary to add that... the apparent vastness and emptiness of the universe, and our insignificant size therein need cause us neither bewilderment nor concern" (*op. cit.* p.143).

To return to Pascal's text and his amendments. Desiring to drive home his arguments, recognizing with George Herbert that "particulars move ever more than the general", he introduces a direct personal touch, changing "le néant d'où tout est tiré et l'infini où tout est englouti" to "il [the man he is thinking of] est tiré... il est englouti". He tightens a slack cord. Who can follow the course of things which spring from nothingness and are lost in infinity? "L'auteur de ces merveilles les comprend et un autre ne le peut faire." That is the first draft. But "un autre" is too vague, so let us write "tout autre", suggesting many previous efforts and vain attempts. Yet man, blind to his disproportion, surrounded, finite creature as he is, on all sides by unfathomable infinity, continues to probe the mystery. Pascal feels inclined to develop further the theme of the little in nature, and begins a paragraph on its difficulty, greater than that of the infinitely great. But there is more to say about man's presumption, as infinite as the object of his search, and this occupies him to the end of the fragment. The reasoning is close and subtle—man's dichotomy, his incapacity to bear extremes, physical or mental, the scientific absurdity of investing material things with spiritual qualities (nature's abhorrence of a vacuum—here a side-thrust at Descartes, etc.)— but there are passages of high and daring poetry, too daring for Port-Royal; and of imitative harmony where an almost physical sensation is conveyed of the crash of solid buildings in a gaping earthquake: "Nous voguons sur un milieu vaste, toujours incertains et flottants, poussés d'un bout à l'autre. Quelque terme où nous pensions nous attacher et nous affermir, il branle [first draft: éloigne] et nous quitte; et si nous le suivons il échappe à nos prises, nous glisse et fuit d'une fuite éternelle"; "Tout notre fondement craque, et le terre ouvre jusqu'aux abîmes" (fr. 72).

The fragment is not complete. A fine concluding summary is ruthlessly sacrificed, and Pascal ends by a promise of two last considerations, which he does not fulfil. The thoughts expressed are not all absolutely original. The notion of the infinitely little was a common-place of the time; that of the sphere whose centre is everywhere and the circumference nowhere is probably as old as Empedocles and was employed by Rabelais, Silhon, and Pierre Bérulle.[19] The comparison was, however, by them applied to God. Pascal, with greater discretion and sense of its material character, more appropriately applies it to God's creation, Nature.

Now take another passage of lighter character which discloses even more patently Pascal's careful choice of words, his irony, his dramatic instinct, his originality—the picture of the solemn magistrate who is led to laugh in church by the grotesqueness of the preacher (fr. 82). It is a little canvas à la Hogarth, where the broad humour is refined by a "faire" of minute and accurate details, chosen with the utmost care.

The "Sénateur" of the first draft, a general term, is reserved for the climax. The personage is a magistrate, a "président à mortier", known for qualities of head and heart, not merely of unruffled but of solid and unshakable reason ("égalité" becomes "solidité de sa raison") and of profound Christian feeling ("ardeur de sa charité"): "charité" rather than "foi" for the sake of the rhythm and to give a touch of unction.

Poetry replaces prose: "vieillesse vénérable" instead of "une mine grave". Place and time are exactly noted. It is not merely a church, but a church at sermon-time, where the magistrate settles down to hear with a reverent attention valuable not only for himself but for the rest of the congregation. Therefore his attitude must be not only marked by "tout le respect dont il est capable", nor merely "un respect plein et sincère", but edifying to behold—"exemplaire".

Enter the preacher. Pascal begins by a description: "la barbe mal faite". But he must be brought on to the stage; so "il monte en chaise", but even before the phrase is completed it gives way to a verb which suggests a jack-in-the-box. So "que le prédicateur vienne à paraître". Then the figure of fun contrasted with the solemnity of the message which breaks down the gravity of the Senator. The sudden spasm of laughter is conveyed by an anacolouthon: "Je parie la perte de gravité de notre Sénateur."

It is amusing to see how Port-Royal handled the passage. Laughter in church seemed irreverent, so the magistrate is set on his bench, the priest becomes a barrister, and the humour of the situation vanishes, for there is nothing unusual in a judge being amused by what happens in court.

Before leaving the question of Pascal's practice of revision in view of publication, we must glance at the fragments headed "A.P.R.; A.P.R. pour demain", which, as already indicated, refer almost certainly to the lecture at Port-Royal, and which incidentally raise a doubt as to the accuracy of Étienne Périer's assertion that the speech on this occasion was "sans avoir été prémédité ou travaillé".

There are two such fragments; the first (fr. 416) being a summary statement of an apparently insoluble problem; the second (fr. 430) taking the form of a *prosopopeia* wherein the Wisdom of God speaks and declares the only possible solution.

Fr. 416, "Grandeur et misère", is a closely reasoned argument, establishing the fact of man's contrasted greatness and misery, but leaving the reader or hearer in complete perplexity as to the cause. It is a forcible piece, with its deliberate reiteration of the word "conclure" (five times in eight consecutive lines), its economy of phrase, and its strong antithesis. It is swift, unhesitating, written *currente calamo*.

Fr. 430 gives us two separate redactions of the utterance of personified Wisdom, of which the second (*b*) "C'est en vain, ô hommes..." is, I

believe, anterior to the first (a) "N'attendez point ni
vérité ni consolation des hommes", and looks like
a preliminary draft, being full of corrections, cancels,
and a set of notes for subsequent development. The
contrast between the two schools of Epicureans and
Stoics put into the mouth of Wisdom in (b) is in (a)
more appropriately assigned to the writer, and the
whole of the *prosopopeia* is declamatory rather than
dialectical. The words are Pascal's, but the thought
is Jansen's or Saint Cyran's, that of man's felicity in
his first state of innocence and of enslavement to the
senses after the Fall.

It is a curious passage, better calculated, one would
think, to please the Jansenist audience than to turn
the heart of the libertine to whom it is addressed. But
that Pascal set store by the rhetorical device is shewn
by his double effort; and it must be remembered
that Frenchmen of all periods are more responsive
to rhetoric, to the *tirade*, than we are. As rhetoric
(a) is highly effective: "J'ai créé l'homme saint,
innocent, parfait; je l'ai rempli de lumière et d'intelligence; je lui ai communiqué ma gloire et mes
merveilles. L'œil de l'homme voyait alors la majesté
de Dieu."

The *prosopopeia* of (b) is more laboured, and it is
interrupted by a reply to the free-thinker's objections
that the divine is incomprehensible and that the

union of God with man is incredible. The reply to
the first objection was probably intended to precede
the *prosopopeia* ("Commencement; après avoir
expliqué l'incompréhensible") in whatever was the
final form adopted. Either *prosopopeia* exhibits
Pascal's mastery of his instrument. In (*b*) the Day
of Wrath is described with a rush and clatter that
strikes both ear and eye; upon it follows a smooth,
flowing movement that reflects the peace and beauty
of Christ's first coming: "...Il paraîtra au dernier
jour avec un tel éclat de foudres et un tel renverse-
ment de la nature que les morts ressuscités et les plus
aveugles le verront. Ce n'est pas en cette sorte qu'il
a voulu paraître dans son avènement de douceur",
etc. Here is the imitative harmony which is the note
of great poetry, and I imagine that the phrase would
have found a place somewhere in the Apology if not
in the *prosopopeia* as finally fixed. It is indeed too
good to be sacrificed.

It is now time, having seen something of the
"effets", to consider the "raisons", i.e. the principles by which Pascal works, and his technique.

The principles, which are obvious, and indeed
elementary, are set forth in a series of fragments
forming section I of Brunschvicg's edition, and in
the *Art de persuader*. This piece, as I have said, is a
kind of appendix to the *De l'esprit géométrique* of

uncertain date, but plainly belonging to the last decade of Pascal's life when he was working for Port-Royal. In both treatises geometry holds the field, for Pascal was especially concerned with teaching how to think clearly. But he admits that clear thought, although an indispensable instrument of persuasion, is not the sole and only instrument, for man has a heart as well as a mind, and the heart, the emotional element in human nature, demands "agrément". Man wishes to be pleased as well as to be logically convinced. Nay, unfortunately, he desires it more. Now there are certain sure rules for procuring intellectual conviction, and Pascal, the mathematician, has no difficulty in marshalling these—rules for careful definition, for the way to accept axioms, for the establishment of proof—which he sums up in two principles, "définir tous les noms qu'on impose; prouver tout, en substituant mentalement les définitions à la place des définis".

But he can give no rules for procuring "agrément". The principles of pleasure are as many and various as the different kinds of men, and as the moods of each man at different periods of his life. To get down to them you must have profound knowledge of human nature and real sympathy.

We do not need the assertion of Dr Besoigne, author of a history of Port-Royal, that Pascal,

through his study of man's heart, knew all its secret
springs and could use his knowledge in justly pro-
portioned speech.[20] We do not need the evidence of
Mme Périer that her brother combined with natural
eloquence and a marvellous facility of saying what
he wanted to say, certain canons of style which
enabled him to say it in the way he would. We
cannot doubt the truth of Nicole's remark that
Pascal was an unrivalled master of the art of true
rhetoric.[21] For we know that like true morality true
rhetoric is a matter of the heart as well as of the head.
But it behoves us to ask what for Pascal were the
rules of that rhetoric; and the answer is easy. There
are none. "True eloquence despises eloquence...it
has no rules." "Eloquence which persuades by
pleasant methods, not by authority like a tyrant, not
like a king", not by exercise of law and order but by
swift, unexpected, arbitrary action.[22]

This insistence on the element of pleasure in
eloquence, even when hedged by an equal insistence
on the need of truth—"Il faut de l'agréable et du
réel: mais il faut que cet agréable soit lui-même pris
du vrai" (fr. 25)—cannot have met with favour at
Port-Royal. "Ces messieurs", with the exception
of Robert d'Andilly, who "cherchait l'agrément
plutôt que l'exactitude", shunned the charm of the
siren. They were indeed incapable of it. M. de Saci,

author of the *Enluminures* which so offended Pascal's
taste, defends them and himself, quite unnecessarily,
from the charge of lightness: "Je sais bien que je n'ai
pas affecté ni les agréments ni les curiosités qu'on
aime dans le monde. Dieu m'est témoin combien
ces afféteries m'ont toujours été en horreur."
M. Hamon was under no illusion as to the jejuneness
of his own style: "J'admirais qu'on pût goûter rien
de ce que j'écrivais: mon style ordinaire est ridicule."

Nicole, of whom Mme de Sévigné could say that
he was of the same stuff as Pascal, judged himself
with a fairer and less favourable eye: "Comme il y a
des peintres qui, ayant peu d'imagination, donnent
à tous leurs personnages le même air, il y a aussi des
gens qui écrivent toujours du même air, et dont
l'allure est toujours reconnaissable. Personne n'eut
jamais plus ce défaut que moi."[23]

Pascal, though he saw the need of charm in the
practice of persuasion, regarded it as a concession to
our animal nature: "pleasure is the coin for which
we will do anything."[24]

He was contemptuous of poetry of which the
elusive characteristic is "agrément".[25] In this he is
patently wrong. Poetry is notoriously difficult to
define, but one may safely say that it includes the
effort to give rhythmical expression to strong
emotion.

If this be so, then Pascal, in a time when strong emotion was singularly absent from verse, was an authentic poet, and most poetical when he drew his inspiration from the book which above all else he valued and studied, the Bible.

Take for instance the meditation which goes by the name of *Le mystère de Jésus* (fr. 553): "Jésus souffre dans sa passion les tourments que lui font les hommes; mais dans l'agonie il souffre les tourments qu'il se donne à lui-même...Jésus est dans un jardin, non de délices comme le premier Adam, où il se perdit et tout le genre humain, mais dans un de supplices, où il s'est sauvé et tout le genre humain."

Pascal, by a great effort of imagination and passionate devotion, stands or kneels by the Sufferer in the garden. He is there; he feels it all. He hears the divine voice, speaking words of comfort, and he answers with confession and surrender. Apart from the mystical rapture of the piece, it is high and undoubted poetry.

And after the New Testament, the Old. When Pascal in the course of his lecture at Port-Royal came to speak of the prophets, he transported his audience, Filleau de la Chaise tells us, by his interpretation of their obscurities. And we can well believe it. For there is among the prophetic fragments which have come down to us one particular masterpiece (fr.726)[26] founded on Isaiah xlix, the Suffering Servant passage: "In meditatione exardescet ignis." As Pascal reads, his imagination is fired, and, translating the Vulgate with freedom, breadth of movement and fullness of expression, he produces something as worthy of the original as our Authorized Version: "Écoutez, peuples éloignés, et vous, habitants des îles de la mer.... Écoutez-moi, vous qui suivez la justice et qui cherchez le Seigneur", etc.

I have already mentioned the *prosopopeia*, the method of personification as dear to the Hebrews as it was to the Babylonians or the Greeks, and especially palatable to his French hearers. But besides translation and imitation there is a further feature of Hebrew poetry, the parallelism which gives it its peculiar force and rhythmical music. This was congenial to Pascal's genius, and the practice of it colours many pages of his prose.

It is easy to collect instances; I cite at hazard from the *Pensées*:

> "S'il se vante, je l'abaisse;
> S'il s'abaisse, je le vante;
> Et le contredis toujours
> Jusqu'à ce qu'il comprenne
> Qu'il est un monstre incompréhensible"
>
> (fr. 420).

"Il veut être grand,
  Et il se voit petit;
  Il veut être heureux,
  Et il se voit misérable;
  Il veut être parfait,
  Et il se voit plein d'imperfections.
Il veut être l'objet de l'amour et de l'estime des
  hommes,
Et il voit que ses défauts ne méritent que leur
  aversion et leur mépris" (fr. 100).

"Plusieurs choses certaines sont contredites,
  Plusieurs fausses passent sans contradiction.
  Ni la contradiction n'est marque de fausseté,
  Ni l'incontradiction n'est marque de vérité"
                                 (fr. 384).

"Nous ne nous tenons jamais au temps présent.
      Nous anticipons l'avenir,
      Comme trop lent à venir
      Pour hâter son cours;
  Ou nous rappelons le passé,
      Pour l'arrêter
      Comme trop prompt;
Si imprudents que nous errons dans les temps qui ne
  sont pas nôtres,
  Et ne pensons point au seul qui nous appartient;
Et si vains que nous ne songeons à ceux qui ne sont
  plus rien,
  Et échappons sans réflexion le seul qui subsiste"
                                 (fr. 172).

"Elle [l'imagination] ne peut rendre sages les fous;
    Mais elle les rend heureux,
    A l'envi de la raison qui ne peut rendre ses amis que
            misérables
        L'une les couvrant de gloire
        L'autre de honte" (fr. 82).

"Il n'est pas honteux à l'homme
    De succomber sous la douleur;
    Et il lui est honteux
    De succomber sous le plaisir" (fr. 160).

And from rhetorical passages in the *Provinciales*:

"Les injures que vous me dîtes
    N'éclairciront pas nos différends,
    Et les menaces que vous me faites en tant de façons
    Ne m'empêcheront pas de me défendre"
                                    (*Lettre* xii).

"Il y a deux peuples et deux mondes
    Répandus sur toute la terre, selon S. Augustin:
    Le monde des enfants de Dieu
    Qui forme un corps
    Dont Jésus Christ est le chef et le roi,
    Et le monde ennemi de Dieu,
    Dont le diable est le chef et le roi" (*Lettre* xiv).

"Ainsi l'on ne me blâmera point
    D'avoir détruit la créance
    Qu'on pouvait avoir en vous,
    Puis qu'il est bien plus juste

De conserver à tant de personnes
Que vous avez décréées
La réputation de piété
Qu'ils ne méritent pas de perdre,
Que de vous laisser la réputation de sincérité
Que vous ne méritez pas d'avoir" (*Lettre* xv).

To descend to details of language and syntax. Pascal's motto lies in words attributed to him which, if they are not his *ipsissima verba*, certainly describe his practice:

"Ce n'est pas assez qu'une chose soit belle; il faut qu'elle soit propre au sujet, qu'il n'y ait rien de trop, ni rien de manque." [27]

"Rien de trop, ni rien de manque"! He had a Greek sense of proportion, and his handling of the language, the strong yet pliable language of his day, declares it "Rien de trop". With this in view he admits nothing into his phrase which it can do without. Hence the frequent omission of the article, both definite and indefinite, and that not only in fragments which are clearly notes for further development hereafter, e.g.

"Curiosité n'est que vanité" (fr. 152).

"Contradiction est une mauvaise marque de vérité....Ni la contradiction n'est marque de fausseté ni l'incontradiction n'est marque de vérité" (fr. 384).

"Pensée fait la grandeur de l'homme" (fr. 346).

"Hasard donne les pensées; et hasard les ôte" (fr. 370).

"Grandeur de l'homme dans sa concupiscence même" (fr. 402).

"Ont toujours bonne espérance" (fr. 182).

He suppresses the complement of the verb and thus gains a singular force and terseness: "Que l'imagination passe outre : elle se lassera plutôt de concevoir que la nature de fournir" (fr. 72). How forceful and concise is seen if we attempt a translation: "It will sooner exhaust the power of conception than nature that of supplying material for conception."

He omits the partitive article:

"Elle ne peut causer ni d'enflure ni d'enfoncement."

"Je ne vois point que nous puissions avoir de scrupule."

"A mesure qu'on a plus de lumière, on découvre plus de grandeur et plus de bassesse dans l'homme."

He omits the antecedent before the relative:

"Qui aurait trouvé le secret de se réjouir du bien."

"Qui voudrait connaître à plein la vanité de l'homme."

"Car qui ne mourrait pour conserver son honneur, celui-là serait infame."

"Qui la [la coutume] ramène à son principe, l'anéantit."

In all this he is not an innovator, but availing himself to the full of current practice; but he also boldly invents new words or uses familiar words in an unusual sense: "tuable", "demi-pécheurs", "niaiser", "fort" (in the sense of strength), "capable" (in the sense of able to communicate with), "apparence"=ἐπιφάνεια, "sensible appearance", "superbe"="orgueil", "médiocrité"= "mediocritas", "montre"="parade", "appareil" ="environment".

Above all "le cœur", to which, besides the sense of the inner depth of human nature, of the seat of knowledge and will with which the Bible provided him, Pascal adds a meaning of his own. For him the heart is that element in man which is other than, contrary to, reason, and which may be summarily described as intuition.

Armed with this rich vocabulary and a singularly elastic grammar, mindful of Montaigne and his preference for a style "tel sur le papier qu'à la bouche", Pascal sets out to build his sentence, his paragraph, his period, his tirade, his fly-sheet. According to his need and the occasion of his utterance, the phrase will be rapid, glittering, epigrammatic, or sinuous and complex; the pleading will be subtle or emotional; the invective will pierce like a lance or crush like a hammer; the pamphlet will betray all the devices of rhetoric—irony, comedy, eloquence, argument—packed within a strictly measured space. The result is the *Pensées sur la religion*, the *Lettres écrites à un provincial*, the *Écrit sur la signature*, as literature immortal, and as language, setting the example whereby French prose has become the most perfect vehicle of lucid and persuasive speech which men have used since the days of Plato and Demosthenes.

It is largely in virtue of this quality, this achievement, that Pascal stands where he does in the esteem of readers. Here lies the secret of his appeal and of his great strength.[28]

"Les ouvrages bien écrits seront les seuls qui passeront à la postérite." Thus wrote M. de Buffon in his *Discours de réception* in the Academy. The claim may sound cold, but it is the climax of a series of postulates which place good writing on a very exalted pedestal. It may well be doubted whether the dignified Burgundian noble would have approved the Gascon's praise of the colloquial—indeed he definitely deprecates it. Nor would he have enjoyed the occasional freedom of Pascal's speech which delights us, or the fragmentary character of the *Pensées*.[29] But Pascal survives, and that with something more than a passive existence. He is a living force and to read him is an inspiration precisely because he speaks with the voice of the inspired prophet and poet, seeing the truth with the single eye which receives and radiates the light.

Notes

By *Œuvres* is meant the edition in the series "Grands écrivains de la France", xiv vols. (1904–1914).

CHAPTER I

[1] "Mon frère...voulait savoir la raison de toutes choses; et comme elles ne sont pas toutes connues, lorsque mon père ne les lui disait pas, ou qu'il lui disait celles qu'on allègue d'ordinaires qui ne sont proprement que des défaites, cela ne le contentait pas.... Quand on ne lui disait pas de bonnes raisons, il en cherchait lui-même" (Mme Périer, *Vie de Blaise Pascal*).

[2] E.g. in the "affaire Saint-Ange".

[3] He resented with some violence of expression the attempt of a Rouen clock-maker to "pirate" his arithmetical machine (*Œuvres*, t. i, p. 311), and the accusation that he had himself "appropriated" the experiment of Torricelli (*ib.* t. ii, pp. 478 ff.). He accused, without justification, the same Torricelli of having exploited the discoveries of others concerning the cycloid (*ib.* t. viii, pp. 195 ff.). He was imperious and impatient towards the competitors for the prize which he offered for a correct solution of that curve (*ib.* t. viii, pp. 159 ff.). On the other hand nothing could be more dignified and correct than his readiness to give honour where it is due in scientific experiment; cf. his letter to Ribeyre of 12 July 1651 (*ib.* t. ii, p. 495).

[4] *Vide hic*, pp. 9 ff.

[5] *Vide hic*, pp. 24 ff.

[6] "M. Pascal parlait fortement" (Racine).

[7] Cf. Ch. Urbain, "Un épisode de la vie de J.-P. Camus" in *Revue d'histoire littéraire* (1895), t. ii, pp. 1 ff., and especially E. Jovy, "Pascal et Saint-Ange", no. 1 of his *Études pascaliennes* (J. Vrin, 1927). See also the procès-verbal of the conversations between Saint-Ange and Pascal's friends (*Œuvres*, t. i, pp. 370 ff.).

[8] *Vide supra*, p. 45.

⁹ "Il (Saint-Ange) prouvait par ses raisonnements que le corps de Jésus-Christ n'était pas formé du sang de la Sainte Vierge, mais... d'une autre matière créée exprès" (Mme Périer, *Vie de Blaise Pascal*).

"On lui demanda si Jésus-Christ n'était pas homme comme nous et d'une même nature que nous....Il répondit qu'il était d'une autre espèce que nous, et qu'il faisait une espèce à part, parce qu'il était produit par un autre motif....Il dit pareillement que la Vierge faisait une espèce à part et distincte de celle des autres hommes, à cause qu'elle était produite par un autre motif que le reste des hommes" (*Œuvres*, t. i, pp. 377, 378).

¹⁰ Compare the following statement of Saint-Ange with one of the *Pensées*: "Tous les sentiments mêmes les plus extravagants de tous les anciens philosophes, et les opinions qui semblaient les plus ridicules quand on les considérait détachées des vrais principes étaient néanmoins véritables et paraissaient très conformes à la raison unis aux principe de sa doctrine [i.e. of Saint Augustine] par ce qu'on connaît toujours la vérité et qu'on ne se trompe jamais que n'en connaissant qu'une partie ou en excluant quelque chose que toutes ces vérités néanmoins n'étaient pas reconnaissables étant séparées" (*Œuvres*, t. i, p. 384).

"Il y a donc un grand nombre de vérités, et de foi et de morale, qui semblent répugnantes, et qui subsistent dans un ordre admirable. La source de toutes les hérésies est l'exclusion de quelques unes de ces vérités; et la source de toutes les objections que nous font les hérétiques est l'ignorance de quelques unes de nos vérités. Et d'ordinaire il arrive que, ne pouvant concevoir le rapport de deux vérités opposées, et croyant que l'aveu de l'une enferme l'exclusion de l'autre, ils s'attachent à l'une, ils excluent l'autre et pensent que nous, au contraire. Or, l'exclusion est la cause de leur hérésie; et l'ignorance que nous tenons l'autre, cause leurs objections" (fr. 862).

The thought is identical, though what is obscure in Saint-Ange's reported speech becomes crystal-clear in Pascal's prose.

[11] Cf. *Œuvres*, t. ii, pp. 54 ff.

[12] The correspondence between Noël and Pascal is in *Œuvres*, t. ii, pp. 82 ff., 179 ff. An excellent commentary is supplied by Strowski, *Pascal et son temps*, t. ii, ch. 4.

[13] Cf. Paul Desjardins, *Les règles de l'honnête discussion selon Pascal*, published during the Dreyfus affair, and republished in 1904 in a volume, *La méthode des classiques français, Corneille, Poussin, Pascal*. I have drawn freely from this admirable pamphlet with the consent of my dear friend, who died at Pontigny last April.

[14] Arnauld wrote two *Apologies de M. Jansen*, in 1644 and 1645, answering the attacks of Dr Isaac Hubert, who discovered forty heretical statements in the *Augustinus*.

[15] The Duc de Liancourt, denied absolution at the confessional of Saint-Sulpice in January 1655 on account of his Jansenist sympathies. Cf. Sainte-Beuve, *Port-Royal*, t. iii, pp. 29 ff.

[16] Cf. Arnauld, *Œuvres* (t. xix, pp. 629 ff.). He put in three pieces in Latin: (1) *Epistola et scriptum Ant. Arnaldi ad sacram facultatem parisiensem congregatam die* vii *dec. ann.* 1655, 20 pp.; (2) *Scripti pars altera die* x *dec.* 1655, 6 pp.; (3) *Epistola Ant. Arnaldi et apologeticus alter die* xvii *Jan.* 1656, 60 pp.

[17] Preface to Wendrock's (i.e. Nicole's) translation of the *Provinciales* into Latin 1658. For another account cf. *Port-Royal*, t. iii, pp. 41–43.

[18] Pascal does not hesitate to use it himself in the *Écrits sur la Grâce*.

[19] Cf. *Œuvres*, t. iv, p. 151.

[20] J. Nouet, S.J., in September 1643 denounced from the pulpit of the maison professe de Paris the author of *La fréquente communion* as "un hérésiarque pire que Luther et Calvin", his doctrine as "abominable", his supporters as "des aveugles".

[21] Cf. *Kidnapped*, ch. x.

[22] *An answer to the Provinciall Letters published by the Jansenists under the name of Lewis Montalt against the doctrine of the Jesuits and School divines: made by some fathers of the Society in France*, Paris, 1659.

[23] Why did Pascal cease writing? Various answers have been

given. By M. Gazier, *Les derniers jours de Blaise Pascal* (1911): Pascal was pricked in conscience and desired to be at peace with all men at Eastertide (1 April 1657). By M. Jovy, *Pascal inédit* (1911), t. ii, p. 30: Pascal was weary of controversy and his deep-set loyalty towards king and Pope was touched by the open hostility of both authorities. By M. Lanson, *Revue d'histoire littéraire* (1901): Pascal was prepared to encourage resistance to Alexander VII's Bull "Ad Sanctam", which the Assembly of Clergy on 14 March 1657 ordered to be published. This Bull reaffirmed the "Cum occasione" of Innocent X, and fixed the "question de fait." A fresh formulary was threatened, requiring explicit adherence to the condemnation of Jansen and his book. But Port-Royal preferred to play "Gallican liberties" against Papal aggression and was manœuvring to get Parlement to refuse registration of the Bull, and Pascal agreed to hold his hand. I used to think M. Jovy's solution the right one; but now I incline to M. Lanson's, which suits all the circumstances.

24 Cf. *Lettre* xvi.

25 Cf. Fontaine, *Mémoires pour servir à l'histoire de Port-Royal*, t. iii, p. 190 (ed. of 1753).

26 Cf. "Sachez que leur objet n'est pas de corrompre les mœurs: ce n'est pas leur dessein. Mais ils n'ont pas aussi pour unique but celui de les réformer. Ce serait une mauvaise politique. Voilà quelle est leur pensée. Ils ont assez bonne opinion d'eux-mêmes pour croire qu'il est utile et comme nécessaire au bien de la religion que leur crédit s'étende partout et qu'ils gouvernent toutes les consciences." The irony is indeed bitter.

27 Cf. Bossuet, *Oraison funèbre de N. Cornet*.

28 For the story of the "tronc de S. Merri" *vide Lettre* xvii and note *ad loc.* of my edition of the *Provinciales* (Manchester, 1920).

29 Cf. *Vie de Blaise Pascal*.

30 This is what the Port-Royal editors substituted for Pascal's word-play: "Je vous laisse cependant dans la liberté de tenir pour le mot de *prochain*, car je vous aime trop pour vous persécuter sous ce prétexte."

31 For Dicastillus and his list of distinguished Jesuits *vide Lettre* xv.

[32] *Lettre* v.

[33] Cf. Abbé Maynard, *Les Provinciales . . . et leur réfutation* (1851), t. i, p. 47.

[34] *Lettre* XII.

[35] The Fourth Lateran Council (1215) required confession to the parish priest at least once a year on the part of all baptized persons.

[36] For Père Daniel, cf. Sainte-Beuve, *Port-Royal*, t. iii, pp. 51 ff.

[37] Cf. "L'abbé: Tout y est, pureté dans le langage, noblesse dans les pensées, solidité dans les raisonnements, finesse dans les railleries, et partout un agrément que l'on ne trouve guère ailleurs", etc., *Parallèles des anciens et des modernes*, seconde partie, troisième Dialogue.

[38] "Mais voici une insigne extravagance et un gros péché mortel contre la raison" (*Lettre* XVI).

[39] "La parole de Dieu étant infaillible dans les faits mêmes, et le rapport des gens et de la raison agissant dans leur étendue étant certains aussi, il faut que ces deux vérités s'accordent" (*Lettre* XVIII).

[40] There were two *Écrits sur la signature*, of which one survives (*Œuvres*, t. x, pp. 171 ff.). The other and longer one was only to be published if the nuns of Port-Royal gave way and signed the Formulary, which they did not. Cf. *Holiness of Pascal*, pp. 19 ff.

[41] For Jacqueline's letter, cf. *Œuvres*, t. x, pp. 103–112 and *Holiness of Pascal*, p. 18.

[42] "Si la vérité était pour vous" writes Blaise in the sixteenth letter, "elle combattrait pour vous, elle vaincrait pour vous; et quelques ennemis que vous eussiez, la vérité vous en délivrerait, selon sa promesse."

[43] Cf. *Lettre* XV.

[44] Cf. "Je viens d'apprendre que celui que tout le monde faisait auteur de vos apologies les désavoue et se fâche qu'on les lui attribue. Il a raison, et j'ai eu tort de l'en avoir soupçonné" (*Lettre* XVI *ad fin.*).

CHAPTER II

[1] Boswell, s. d. 15 February 1766.

[2] Cf. Clement C. J. Webb, *Pascal's philosophy of religion* (Oxford, 1929).

[3] Cf. "Les Provinciales ont tué la scolastique en morale, comme Descartes y a coupé court en métaphysique" (*Port-Royal*, t. iii, p. 259).

[4] "Jesuita" = hypocrite is found in Germany before the foundation of Loyola's society. Cf. Brou, *Les Jésuites de la légende* (1906), t. i, p. 25.

[5] Cf. a good chapter on "the reign of bad taste" in A. Tilley's *From Montaigne to Molière* (2nd ed. Cambridge, 1900).

[6] The most signal example of Jesuit ornamentation is the church of St Michael's, Louvain.

[7] E.g. the *Imago primi saeculi societatis Jesu* (Antwerp, 1640), which has been condemned for its want of taste even by friends of the Society. Cf. A. Brou, *Les Jésuites de la légende* (1906), t. i, p. 364.

[8] Cf. Tilley, *op. cit.* p. 191.

[9] "Il faut qu'on n'en puisse dire ni: 'il est mathématicien' ni 'prédicateur', ni 'éloquent', mais 'il est honnête homme'. Cette qualité universelle me plaît seule" (fr. 35).

[10] Letter to Fermat, 10 August 1660 (*Œuvres*, t. x, p. 4).

[11] Cf. "Réponse du Provincial", after perusal of Letters i and ii.

[12] This is the considered opinion of Sainte-Beuve (*Port-Royal*, t. iii, pp. 259 ff.). It is contested by Brunetière in the Introduction to his edition of three *Provinciales* (Hachette), but I think that Sainte-Beuve is right.

[13] "Without challenge." I do not forget the contemptuous description by Méré on the occasion of the trip to Poitou whither he went with the Duc de Roannez and Pascal in 1653 (?) "Le D.D.R. a l'esprit mathématique et, pour ne pas s'ennuyer sur le chemin, il avait fait provision d'un homme entre deux âges, qui n'était alors

que fort peu connu, mais qui depuis a bien fait parler de lui. C'était un grand mathématicien, qui ne savait que cela. Ces sciences ne donnent pas les agréments du monde; et cet homme, qui n'avait ni goût ni sentiment, ne laissait pas de se mêler en tout ce que nous disions, mais il nous surprenait presque toujours et nous faisait souvent rire." Méré goes on to boast how he weaned "cet homme" from his devotion to mathematics and made of him a new man. If the description is true, it is evidence of the ease with which Pascal adapted himself to unwonted surroundings. But I suspect a point of jealousy on the part of Méré.

[14] "Il a mis toute la force de son esprit à connaître et à pratiquer la perfection de la morale chrétienne, à laquelle il a consacré tous les talents que Dieu lui avait donnés" (*Vie de Blaise Pascal*).

[15] Cf. *L'Entretien avec Saci* (*Œuvres*, t. iv, pp. 26 ff.).

[16] Cf. "...le temps où nous sommes, où la corruption de la morale est aux maisons de sainteté et dans les livres des théologiens et des religieux, où elle ne devrait pas être", *Lettre à M. et à Mlle de Roannez*, September 1656 (*Œuvres*, t. v, p. 406).

[17] Cf. "Nous ne connaissons Dieu que par Jésus-Christ. Sans ce médiateur est ôtée toute communication avec Dieu" (fr. 547).

[18] Cf. "La vraie morale se moque de la morale; c'est à dire que la morale du jugement se moque de la morale de l'esprit qui est sans règles" (the relative refers to "la morale du jugement") (fr. 4).

[19] Mme de Sévigné, 26 January 1674.

[20] *Vide supra*, pp. 13 ff.

[21] "Prière pour demander à Dieu le bon usage des maladies" (*Œuvres*, t. ix, pp. 323–340).

[22] Cf. Jacqueline's letter to Blaise of 1 December 1655 (*Œuvres*, t. iv, p. 81) and *Holiness of Pascal*, p. 130.

[23] *Vie de Blaise Pascal*.

[24] Cf. "Frui est amore alicui rei inhaerere propter se ipsam.... Res igitur quibus fruendum est, pater et filius et spiritus sanctus est", Augustine, *De doctrina christiana*, cc. iv, v, and cf. J. Burnaby, *Amor Dei* (1938), pp. 11 f., 104 ff., 130, 167.

²⁵ Cf. Saint-Cyran. *Œuvres chrétiennes*, t. iv, p. 37.

²⁶ *Le mystère de Jésus* (fr. 553).

²⁷ Cf. "Quelle vanité que la peinture, qui attire l'admiration par la ressemblance des choses dont on n'admire point les originaux" (fr. 134). I am reminded of the remark made to Roger Fry by a military man: "What I demand in a picture is that it shall represent to me something which I can recognize at once, and if it doesn't do that I maintain that it is a bad picture" (*Roger Fry, a biography*, by Virginia Woolf (1940), p. 64).

²⁸ Cf. "Je ne puis juger de mon ouvrage en le faisant; il faut que je fasse comme les peintres et que je m'en éloigne" (fr. 114).

²⁹ Cf. fr. 12 and 13.

³⁰ E.g. Professor Alan Boase, *The Fortunes of Montaigne* (1935).

³¹ Cf. E. Droz, *Le scepticisme de Pascal* (1886).

³² Cf. "C'est le consentement de vous à vous-même, et la voix constante de votre raison, et non des autres, qui vous doit faire croire" (fr. 260).

³³ Cf. "La conduite de Dieu, qui dispose toutes choses avec douceur, est de mettre la religion dans l'esprit par les raisons, et dans le cœur par la grâce. Mais de la vouloir mettre dans l'esprit et dans le cœur par la force et par les menaces, ce n'est pas y mettre la religion, mais la terreur, *terrorem potius quam religionem*" (fr. 185).

³⁴ Cf. "Tous les hommes recherchent d'être heureux....La volonté ne fait jamais la moindre démarche que vers cet objet. C'est le motif de toutes les actions de tous les hommes, jusqu'à ceux qui vont se pendre" (fr. 425).

³⁵ Cf. "Nous sommes incapables de ne pas souhaiter la vérité et le bonheur, et sommes incapables ni de certitude ni de bonheur" (fr. 437).

³⁶ Cf. *L'Entretien avec Saci.*

³⁷ Cf. "La vraie nature étant perdue, tout devient sa nature; comme, le véritable bien étant perdu, tout devient son véritable bien" (fr. 426).

³⁸ Cf. "Tout ce qui est au monde est concupiscence de la chair,

ou concupiscence des yeux ou orgueil de la vie; *libido sentiendi, libido sciendi, libido dominandi.*"

[39] Cf. "On a fondé et tiré de la concupiscence des règles admirables de police, de morale et de justice, mais dans le fond, ce vilain fond de l'homme, ce *figmentum malum*, n'est que couvert: il n'est pas ôté" (fr. 453). "Le moi est haïssable: vous, Miton, le couvrez, vous ne l'ôtez pas pour cela" (fr. 455).

[40] "L'Ecclésiaste montre que l'homme sans Dieu est dans l'ignorance de tout, et dans un malheur inévitable. Car c'est être malheureux que de vouloir et ne pouvoir. Or il veut être heureux et assuré de quelque vérité; et cependant il ne peut ni savoir, ni désirer point de savoir. Il ne peut même douter" (fr. 389).

[41] "L'homme n'est donc que déguisement, que mensonge et hypocrisie, et en soi-même et à l'égard des autres" (fr. 100 *ad fin.*).

[42] Conc. Trid. Sess. vi, cap. 1.

[43] Cf. *Lettre à M. et Mlle Roannez*, 24 September 1656 (*Œuvres*, t. v, p. 409).

[44] Cf. "La foi embrasse plusieurs vérités qui semblent se contredire" (fr. 862).

[45] Cf. "Les deux raisons contraires. Il faut commencer par là: sans cela on n'entend rien, et tout est hérétique; et même, à la fin de chaque vérité, il faut ajouter qu'on se souvient de la vérité opposée" (fr. 567).

[46] The story of Nicole's attempt to mitigate the harshness of the authentic Port-Royalist doctrine of Election and Grace is of primary importance in tracing the curve of Pascal's theological and moral development, for he, on Nicole's showing, was closely associated therewith. Four years before his death in 1695 Nicole wrote a *Traité de la Grâce générale*, not published till 1715, which is Augustine seen through Thomism. In the preface Nicole says: "Il y a près de 34 ans [i.e. in 1657–8] qu'ayant eu quelque engagement de m'appliquer aux différends qui partagent les théologiens sur la matière de la Grâce, il me parut que beaucoup d'entre eux étaient choqués plutôt de certains termes qu'ils expliquaient d'une manière odieuse

que des opinions mêmes, ce qui me porta à croire que c'était un devoir de charité et de justice, sans rien changer ni altérer...de tâcher d'adoucir par des expressions favorables ce qui rebutait ces personnes dans la doctrine de Saint-Augustin....J'étais persuadé de plus qu'il n'y avait rien de plus avantageux à la doctrine de S.A. que de lui ôter un air de dureté qui en éloigne bien des gens.... Feu M. Pascal, avec qui j'ai eu le bien d'être très étroitement uni, n'a pas peu aidé à nourrir en moi cette inclination...il disait que s'il avait à traiter cette matière, il espérait de réussir à rendre cette doctrine si plausible et de la dépouiller tellement d'un certain air farouche qu'on lui donne qu'elle serait au goût de toutes sortes d'esprits." Pascal in effect made the attempt with the *Écrits sur la Grâce*, with doubtful success (*vide supra*, p. 51). Nicole's system may be stated under two heads: (1) If men were left to themselves without any supernatural interior grace, they would lack the natural power of observing the commandments and therefore would not be guilty, if they failed to observe them, and (2) as a fact this interior grace, consisting in good thoughts which enlighten the mind, and in good movements which enkindle the will, is bestowed on all men. Hence even the heathen were not necessarily sinful in all their acts, but were accessible to God's Grace and Christ's Redemption.

This was repugnant to Jansenists in general, and in particular to Arnauld, who had written a tract against the so-called virtues of the heathen (*De la nécessité de la foi pour être sauvé*).

How far Nicole went in the direction of Thomism appears from a letter to Quesnel: "Je vous avoue qu'en examinant en cette matière ce qu'on appelle la doctrine des Thomistes sur la Grâce, je suis entré de bonne foi dans ce sentiment, que cette doctrine était la plus conforme aux règles de l'Église."

How far Pascal went with Nicole is open to question, but in view of the last two *Provinciales* and the extremely mild treatment accorded to the Molinists in the *Écrits sur la Grâce*, it may be presumed that he would have gone a good way. Cf. Strowski, *op. cit.* t. iii. ch. 5.

⁴⁷ "Il semblait que M. Pascal était toujours en colère et qu'il voulait jurer." Cf. V. Giraud, *La vie héroïque de Blaise Pascal* (1923), p. 255.

⁴⁸ "Vous êtes donc proprement un roi de concupiscence, votre royaume est de peu d'étendue, mais vous êtes égal en cela aux plus grands rois de la terre. Ils sont comme vous des rois de concupiscence" (*Œuvres*, t. ix, p. 372).

⁴⁹ Cf. "Il avait un si grand zèle pour l'ordre de Dieu qu'il ne pouvait souffrir qu'il fût violé en quoi que ce soit; c'est ce qui le rendait si ardent pour le service du roi qu'il résistait à tout le monde lors les troubles de Paris, et toujours depuis il appelait des prétextes toutes les raisons qu'on donnait pour excuser cette rébellion" (*Vie de Blaise Pascal*).

⁵⁰ "La puissance des rois est fondée sur la raison et sur la folie du peuple, et bien plus sur la folie" (fr. 330).

⁵¹ "Il ne manque jamais d'y avoir auprès des personnes des rois un grand nombre de gens qui veillent à faire succéder le divertissement à leurs affaires, et qui observent tout le temps de leur loisir pour leur fournir des plaisirs et des jeux, en sorte qu'il n'y ait point de vide, c.à.d. qu'ils sont environnés de personnes qui ont un soin merveilleux de prendre garde que le roi ne soit seul et en état de penser à soi, sachant bien qu'il sera misérable, tout roi qu'il est, s'il y pense" (fr. 142).

⁵² "Le peuple a les opinions très saines: ..." (fr. 324); "Il est dangereux de dire au peuple que les lois ne sont pas justes, car il n'y obéit qu'à cause qu'il les croit justes..." (fr. 326), and cf. *supra*, n. 50.

⁵³ Cf. "Le droit à ses époques, l'entrée de Saturne au Lion nous marque l'origine d'un tel crime. Plaisante justice qu'une rivière borne! Vérité au deçà des Pyrénées, erreur au delà" (fr. 294).

⁵⁴ Cf. "Qu'on s'imagine un corps plein de membres pensants" (fr. 473).

⁵⁵ Cf. W. L. Davidson, *The Stoic Creed* (1907), pp. 180 ff.

⁵⁶ Cf. Jovy, *Pascal inédit*, t. ii, pp. 487 ff. and *Holiness of Pascal*, pp. 102 ff.

CHAPTER III

¹ The scene at M. de Lamoignon's when Boileau lost his head and the Jesuit, friend of Bourdaloue, his temper à propos of Pascal is vividly described by Mme de Sévigné in a letter to her daughter of 15 January 1690. It is one of her best letters.

² *Vide supra*, p. 27 and chap. I, n. 44.

³ What they did to the *Provinciales* is seen in a comparison of the second edition (1659) with the original issue of the pamphlets. What they did to the fragments which they issued under the title of *Pensées* raised the ire of Victor Cousin, who in 1842 referred the Academy to the autograph MS. in order to convince themselves of the ill-faith of the editors. But indeed they meant no wrong and believed they were doing a service to Pascal. Brienne the Oratorian wrote to Mme Périer with engaging candour: "Comme ce qu'on y a fait ne change en aucune façon le sens ni les expressions de l'auteur mais ne fait que les éclaircir et les embellir", etc. For an example of their "embellissements" cf. their treatment of the picture of a magistrate in church (*vide supra*, p. 72).

⁴ Cf. "Après ce jugement si précis" (Nicole to the Marquis de Sévigné, *Essais de morale*, t. viii, p. 220 (ed. 1730)), "nous voilà réduits à n'en oser dire notre sentiment, et à faire semblant de trouver admirable ce que nous n'entendons pas....Pour vous dire la vérité, j'ai eu jusques ici quelque chose de ce méchant signe. J'y ai bien trouvé un grand nombre de pierres assez bien taillées et capables d'orner un grand bâtiment, mais le reste ne m'a paru que des matériaux confus, sans que je visse l'usage qu'il en voulait faire. Il y a même quelques sentiments qui ne me paraissent pas tout à fait exacts et qui ressemblent à des pensées hasardées....Je pourrais vous faire plusieurs autres objections sur ces *Pensées* qui me semblent quelquefois un peu trop dogmatiques, et qui incommodent ainsi mon amour-propre, qui n'aime pas à être régenté si fièrement."

[5] Cf. Charles de Sévigné to his mother, quoted by her in a letter of 12 January 1676: "Vous qui aimez tant les bons styles, et qui vous y connaissez si bien...pouvez-vous mettre en comparaison le style de Port Royal avec celui de M. Pascal? C'est celui-là qui dégoûte de tous les autres. M. Nicole met une quantité de belles paroles dans le sien: cela fatigue et fait mal à la fin; c'est comme qui mangerait trop de blanc-manger: voilà ma décision."

[6] Cf. "Je remarquais que vous prétendiez prendre la place de l'auteur des *petites lettres*; mais je remarquais en même temps que vous étiez beaucoup au-dessous de lui et qu'il y avait une grande différence entre une *Provinciale* et une *imaginaire*" (Racine, *Lettre à l'auteur des Hérésies imaginaires et des deux Visionnaires*).

[7] Cf. "On parla des ouvrages des anciens et des modernes; Despréaux soutint les anciens, à la réserve d'un seul moderne qui surpassait, à son goût, et les vieux et les nouveaux" (Mme de Sévigné, in the letter referred to, *supra*, n. 1).

[8] Cf. "Ce dernier écrit [viz. the *Pensées*] a surpassé ce que j'attendais d'un esprit que je croyais le plus grand qui eût paru en notre siècle; et si je n'ose pas dire que saint Augustin aurait eu peine à égaler ce que je vois, par les fragments, que M. Pascal pouvait faire, je ne saurais dire qu'il eût pu le surpasser: au moins je ne vois que ces deux que l'on puisse comparer l'un à l'autre" (Le Nain de Tillemont to Étienne Périer).

[9] Cf. Rapin, *Mémoires*, t. i, p. 211.

[10] Cf. M. Hervier, *Les écrivains français jugés par leurs contemporains* (2de edition, pp. 152 ff.)

[11] E.g. the famous excuse: "Je n'ai fait celle-ci plus longue que parce que je n'ai pas eu le temps de la faire plus courte", is an echo of a phrase of the *Socrate chrétien*. The *Pensées* supply evidence of other borrowings from Balzac, e.g. "Il n'est pas permis au plus équitable homme du monde d'être juge en sa cause. J'en sais qui pour ne pas tomber dans cet amour-propre ont été les plus injustes du monde à contre-biais" (fr. 82), which is a "raccourci" of a long paragraph of Balzac's *Aristippe*. "J'ai vu de ces faux justes deçà et delà les monts. J'en ai vu qui pour faire admirer leur intégrité...

prenaient l'intérêt d'un étranger contre celui d'un parent ou d'un ami". "Il n'est ni ange ni bête, mais homme" (fr. 140). "L'homme n'est ni ange ni bête, et le malheur veut que qui veut faire l'ange fait la bête" (fr. 358) derive either from Montaigne, III, 13 or from Balzac: "L'homme est fait d'un Dieu et d'une bête qui sont attachés ensemble" (*Dissertation au R. P. Domandre*). And Balzac supplies the simile of village queens (*Socrate chrétien*) which Pascal uses in fr. 33: "Nous appelons les sonnets faits sur ce modèle-là les reines de village."

[12] Cf. "Il ne voulait pas qu'on s'amusât à épiloguer sur les paroles, et à être plus longtemps à peser les mots qu'un avaricieux ne serait à peser l'or à son trébuchet" (Lancelot, *Mémoires de Saint Cyran*, t. ii, p. 130).

[13] Cf. "Pour mériter cet éloge infini et sans bornes que Perrault a donné aux Provinciales, il ne suffit pas qu'il n'y ait ni solécismes ni barbarismes. Une petite pièce de cette nature ne passe point pour un chef-d'œuvre, si on y trouve autant de fautes qu'il y a de pages", etc. (*Sixième Entretien de Cléandre et d'Eudoxe* (1694)).

[14] E.g. Charles Du Bos, in his eloquent article "Le langage de Pascal" (*Revue hebdomadaire* for 14 July 1923), in many respects an admirable article, speaks of "l'expression pascalienne—surgissant telle un bloc de formation primitive, chauffé du dedans, dont l'irradiation même est étroitement liée aux calories qu'il dégage—semble toujours antérieur à ces plans de l'espace et du temps sur lesquels se poursuivent, s'accomplissent les opérations qui engendrent les grands styles." This, in view of Pascal's frequent elaboration, seems to me too general.

[15] Cf. "Il paraît de là que, quoi que ce soit qu'on veuille persuader, il faut avoir égard à la personne à qui on en veut, dont il faut connaître l'esprit et le cœur, quels principes il accorde, quelles choses il aime; et ensuite remarquer, dans la chose dont il s'agit, quels rapports elle a avec les principes avoués ou avec les objets délicieux par les charmes qu'on lui donne" (*Art de persuader*).

[16] Cf. *The Holiness of Pascal*, pp. 52 ff.

[17] Cf. E. Jovy, *Études pascaliennes*, t. viii, "Les antécédents de 'l'infiniment petit' dans Pascal" (Vrin, 1932).

[18] *Pensées de Pascal*, t. i, p. 15.

[19] *Œuvres*, t. xii, p. 27 n.

[20] *Vide infra*, n. 27.

[21] "Feu M. Pascal, qui savait autant de véritable rhétorique que personne en ait jamais su" (*Logique de Port Royal*, 3ᵉ partie, § 6).

[22] "Éloquence qui persuade par douceur, non par empire, en tyran, non en roi" (fr. 15). Pascal distinguishes between the constitutional rule of the king and the arbitrary rule of the tyrant in fr. 310, 311.

[23] Cf. Nicole, *Nouvelles lettres* (ed. 1735), L. LVI.

[24] Cf. "Tant la malice de la concupiscence se plaît à faire tout le contraire de ce qu'on veut obtenir de nous sans nous donner du plaisir, qui est la monnaie pour laquelle nous donnons tout ce qu'on veut" (fr. 24).

[25] "On ne sait pas en quoi consiste l'agrément, qui est l'objet de la poésie" (fr. 33).

[26] Cf. Havet, *Pensées de Pascal*, p. xxxix.

[27] The fragment (15) from which this paragraph is taken is a summary of Pascal's practice by Dr Besoigne (*vide supra*, p. 76) founded on Mme de Périer's *Vie* and Pascal's own words in the *Art de persuader* and reproduced by Bossut in his edition of the *Pensées* (1779). Cf. Brunschvicg's note, *ad loc.*

[28] As I go to press, my eye, guided by Mr Desmond Mac-Carthy (*Sunday Times*, Dec. 8) falls upon one of Mr L. Pearsall-Smith's thoughts (*More Trivia*, 1922) entitled "Phrases", which confirms me in my opinion. "Is there", he writes, "any solace like the solace and consolation of Language? When I am disconcerted by the unpleasing aspects of existence...it is not in Metaphysics nor in Religion that I seek for reassurance, but in fine phrases...."

[29] Cf. "Ceux qui écrivent comme ils parlent, quoiqu'ils parlent très bien, écrivent mal.... Ceux qui craignent de perdre des pensées isolées, fugitives et qui ecrivent en différents temps des morceaux détachés ne les réunissent jamais sans transitions forcées" (*Discours de réception*, 1753).

Some important books and articles on Pascal which have appeared during the last twenty years.

CHEVALIER, J. *Pascal* (Paris, Plon, 1922).
—— *Pensées.* 2 vols. (Paris, Gabalda, 1925).
BREMOND, H. *En prière avec Pascal* (Paris, Bloud et Gay, 1923).
LAPORTE J. *Pascal et Port-Royal* (*Rev. de métaph. et de morale,* 1923).
—— *Le cœur et la raison* (*Rev. philosophique,* 1927).
Revue hebdom. (1923. Art. by Blondel, L. Brunschvicg, Chevalier, Laporte, Rauh).
BAUDIN. *L'Originalité de Pascal* (Strasbourg, *Rev. des sciences relig.* 1924).
BRUNSCHVICG, L. *Le génie de Pascal* (Paris, Hachette, 1924).
—— *Pascal* (Paris, Rieder, 1932).
SOLTAU, R. *Pascal, the man and the message* (London, 1927).
JOVY, E. *Études pascaliennes,* 9 vols. (Paris, Vrin, 1927–32).
MAURIAC, F. *Blaise Pascal et sa sœur Jacqueline* (Paris, Hachette, 1931).
LHERMET, J. *Pascal et la Bible* (Paris, Vrin, 1931). But see review by A. Dedieu in *R.H.L.* for 1933.
CONSTANTIN, C. Article on Pascal in Vacant and Mangenot's *Dictionnaire de théologie catholique,* t. xi (Paris, Letouzey, 1932).
TOURNEUR, Z. *Beauté poétique* (Melun, 1933).
—— *Pensées.* 2 vols. (critical edition, Paris, ed. Cluny, 1938).
SOREAU, E. *Pascal* (Paris, S.F.E.L.T. 1934).
EASTWOOD, D. M. *The Revival of Pascal* (Oxford, 1936).
BISHOP, M. G. *Pascal: the life of a genius* (London, U.S.A. pr., 1937).
DEDIEU, A. *Pensées et œuvres choisies* (Paris, librairie l'École, 1937).
FALUCCI. *Le problème de la vérité chez Pascal* (Paris, Didier, 1939).
BENZECRI, ED. *L'esprit humain selon Pascal* (Paris, Alcan, 1939; with good bibliography).

INDEX

Italic figures denote references to the Notes

For EU product safety concerns, contact us at Calle de José Abascal, 56–1°, 28003 Madrid, Spain or eugpsr@cambridge.org.

www.ingramcontent.com/pod-product-compliance
Ingram Content Group UK Ltd.
Pitfield, Milton Keynes, MK11 3LW, UK
UKHW012333130625
459647UK00009B/259